DOING THE WORK OF LOVE

To Elly May,
From my heart to your ~
Love on ,

Tom
11/9/03

HARD BLESSINGS
DOING THE WORK OF LOVE

Tom Owen-Towle

SunInk Publications, Carmel, California

(paperback) 9 8 7 6 5 4 3 2 1

HARD BLESSINGS
DOING THE WORK OF LOVE
Original copyright © 1999 by Tom Owen-Towle

contact SunInk Presentations,
37931 Palo Colorado Road, Carmel, California 93923

Tel: (408) 625-0588, Fax: (408) 625-3770
e-mail - sunink@ricmasten.com

Library of Congress Catalogue Card No. 99-095109

ISBN 0-931104-48-3

DEDICATION

To all who doggedly pursue the hard blessings
of loving and being loved...

33 HARD BLESSINGS

INTRODUCTION   iX

I. LOVE BEING DIFFICULT   I

II. KEEP THE GIFT MOVING   5

III. EARTH'S THE RIGHT PLACE   9

IV. NOBODY BUT YOURSELF   I4

V. A POLICY, NOT AN EMOTION   I8

VI. TWIN ARTS   22

VII. THY NEIGHBOR AS THYSELF   24

VIII. EVERY GRAIN OF SAND   27

IX. LIE BACK AND THE SEA WILL HOLD YOU   30

X. GOD IN THE LURKING-PLACES   34

XI. PAYING ATTENTION   38

XII. SHOWING ANGER...EVEN HATE   4I

XIII. WIDENING CIRCLES   45

XIV. EROTIC NOT SEXY   49

XV. YE SHALL RESPECT ONE ANOTHER   54

XVI. DURING THE DRAB INTERVALS   58

XVII. JUST BE MY FRIEND   6I

XVIII. MOST INTENSIVE COURSE   65

XIX. WE MUST PERFORCE GO ALONE   70

XX. CARING IS EVERYTHING   73

XXI. GUILT MATTERS   76

XXII. LET YOUR LAUGHTER RING FORTH   80

XXIII. DANGER TO EVERY REPRESSIVE ORDER   82

XXIV. YOUNG AND OLD TOGETHER   86

XXV. SHAKING HANDS WITH THE DRAGONS   89

XXVI. SURRENDERING   91

XXVII. BLESSED ARE THEY WHO MOURN   94

XXVIII. LISTENING TO THE SILENCES   96

XXIX. THREE REQUIREMENTS   99

XXX. FORGIVENESS   102

XXXI. ALWAYS GREEN AND FULL OF SAP   107

XXXII. SHOUT AMEN   112

XXXIII. STRONGER THAN DEATH   116

APPENDIX: MORE QUOTES TO LIVE BY   119

INTRODUCTION

...I have slowly learned...
that love is hard,
that while many good things are easy, true love is not,
because love is first of all a power,
its own power,
which continually must make its way forward, from night
into day, from transcending union always forward into difficult day.

Galway Kinnell

W ho would dare to write about love! An excess of syrup
and pap has already been penned on the subject. Some
have prudently suggested that we establish a moratorium for
at least a year on a word that has lost its finest meanings for
us. As Aldous Huxley lamented:

Of all the worn, smudged, dog-eared words in our vocabu-
lary, love is surely the grubbiest, smelliest, slimiest. Bawled
from a million pulpits, lasciviously crooned through hun-
dreds of millions of loud speakers, it has become an outrage
to good taste and decent feeling, an obscenity that one hesi-
tates to pronounce. And yet it has to be pronounced, for,
after all, "love" is the last word.

Smudged to be sure, love still remains the last word of existence, the first word, the key word—what philosopher
Gabriel Marcel declared "the essential ontological datum."
Human love must be voiced and embodied, however inad-
equately. Our supreme task during our lifetime is to become

full-fledged lovers on all fronts: loving friends and family; loving strangers, even enemies; loving wild animals and insensate objects; loving the Eternal One; loving creation amid its wondrous plenitude.

A colleague preached a sermon some 25 years ago entitled "Living in a World Running Out of Love." Upon revisiting her homily, she bemoaned: "If anything has altered in the intervening period it is that the supply of human love appeared closer than ever to exhaustion." I can't quarrel with her assessment. While love-substitutes abound in contemporary society, rarely do we experience the genuine article—sturdy affection born of respect and ardor.

Love is our most prostituted concept, yet it remains our most potent reality. While we must "be of love a little more careful than of anything else" (e. e. cummings), we cannot avoid speaking it, singing it, sharing it. Love may not make the world go around as the romantics contend (alas, greed is closer to doing that), but love does, as one sage muses, make the ride worthwhile.

The story goes that Winston Churchill was dining one night at a deluxe restaurant. After a scrumptious repast, he ordered pudding to crown the evening. He found it displeasing and summoned a waiter to his table: "My good sir, the pudding is interesting but clearly lacks a **theme!**" Such is the plight of too many moderns: our lives lack any discernible theme, let alone a fulfilling one. This book contends that loving and being loved should constitute the governing theme of our individual and communal existence. Only love, at its truest, can turn lives around; only love can redeem civilization.

French existentialist Albert Camus put it bluntly: "Absurdity is king, but love saves us from it." And African-American activist Alice Walker phrases it similarly in a recent book: "Anything we truly love can be saved..." Yes, love, when genuinely practiced, carries transformative, even salvational power. Love will enable our 21st-century universe not only to survive, but to flourish. Love alone.

The following essays (remember the word *essay* literally means "an attempt") aspire to evoke, not exhaust, the range of what St. Augustine called "the overlapping loves" we encounter during our earthly trek: parent-child, human-divine, erotic intimacy, friendship, work comradeship, and more. Our culture usually equates love with heterosexual romance. Libraries are teeming with books reflective of that emphasis. But love as a commodious reality charges us to cultivate love of self, neighbor, nature, and God—exploring the staggering array of dimensions that comprise love at its hardest: trust, guilt, forgiveness, compromise, weeping, anger, and loneliness.

Writers have waxed lyrical about love throughout the centuries. They have also satirized it, alleging "love is simply an intoxication of the nervous system," or "love is like the measles—we can have it but once, and the later in life we have it, the tougher it goes with us." Plato, at one point, had the gall to label love "a grave mental disease."

Although much of love is laughable or downright foolish, the reality transcends amusement. In exploring the hard blessings of love, one must prove serious without turning grim, blithesome without sounding farcical, tender without becoming maudlin.

Zen Buddhist John Tarrant seems to grasp love's fierce, twisting nature:

> *Like the stars over dark fields, love is the gift of the eternal forces. We do not know why it appears; it is just the song the universe sings to itself. And, like other beauties, it is a demanding guest. As soon as love arrives, we have to serve it—we were naked and now must put on clothes and work.*

Yea, the blessings of love are hard—usually complex, sometimes onerous, even harsh. Difficult yet welcome gifts. The "true love" to which the poet Kinnell refers is the outcome of both grit and grace...hard-earned from within and bestowed from beyond.

HARD BLESSINGS
DOING THE WORK OF LOVE

LOVE BEING DIFFICULT

To love is good, too: love being difficult. For one human being to love another: that is perhaps the most difficult of all our tasks, the ultimate, the last test and proof, the work for which all other work is but preparation.

Rainer Maria Rilke

Now take the chisel and make for the bone!
Difficult love, you are the sculptor here.
The image you must wrest, great and severe.

May Sarton

There is no solution, therefore, let us pursue it lovingly.

Harold Mitchell

For fresh insight on the weather-beaten and much-maligned virtue called love, let's revisit the poetic acumen of Rainer Maria Rilke: "To love is good, too: love being difficult." He goes on to observe that robust loving means "always holding to the difficult..." Rilke knew that the only version of love worth pursuing must prove hardy and discerning, not insipid and promiscuous.

"Love being difficult" would exact tough choices rather than indulgent gestures, arousing us to celebrate life fiercely even while consenting to die gracefully. Love summons us to share our bodies respectfully and exercise our consciences sagely. Love excludes certain behaviors in service of a healthier embrace. Love, according to Rilke, holds unerringly to what is difficult—not impossible, or necessarily dangerous, but unfailingly strenuous.

Rilke's all too brief life (1875-1926) comprised an ode to love and its attendant obstacles. Although he matured to stand among the greatest of European lyric poets writing in the years that bordered 1900, Rainer Maria Rilke struggled mightily in his own personal life. He readily confessed to being "inept at life."

Rilke recalls "an anxious, heavy childhood." The child of a loveless marriage, his mother refused to acknowledge her son's gender, dressing him "like a big doll" in girl's clothing as a young boy. She did so, mourning the loss of her preceding pregnancy of a baby girl. The suffocating care of Rilke's mother led to physical hypersensitivity, adding to the instability of his self-esteem. While admiring the sincerity of his civil-servant father, a deep abyss separated them, for the latter was a stiff, uncommunicative man, who endured a lackluster occupation as a railroad official and could comprehend neither his son's temperament nor his poetry.

Constantly ill as a youngster and dogged by depression throughout his days, Rainer took refuge early on in a rich fantasy life, the wellspring for his evocative and sensual poetry.

Although as an adult Rilke was attracted to a bevy of older women who tended to mother him, he practiced his vision of an emancipated, mature marriage but briefly—to sculptor, Clara Westhoff. Believing that "art was the means whereby the solitary person would fulfill himself," and plagued with financial problems, Rilke soon abandoned family life and contrived an existence dedicated to the egocentric, somewhat rootless, pathway of the artist. While his relational life proved futile, Rilke's poetic refrains plumbed erotic depths.

If Rilke's associations with women were unsatisfying, his unconventional encounters with God were beguiling. "I circle around God, around the primordial tower. I've been circling for thousands of years and I still don't know: Am I a falcon, a storm, or a great song?" Such a description of his fleeting connection with the Eternal resembled his ties with both women and men. Rilke clearly found ultimate solace and nourishment in the company of his own being.

Although Rilke's own love life was deficient, he never lost confidence in the human capacity to save the world through love. His clear-sighted words on the subject furnish inspirational guidance as we near the threshold of the 21st century. Love manifests the central good of human existence, precisely because it is challenging to comprehend and confounding to embody. Love undoubtedly is our "most difficult" and "ultimate" human task. The forthcoming century, even more severely than Rilke's world, will tempt us into choosing the thrill of infatuation or the solace of symbiosis rather than adhering to love's unbending directives.

Yet Rilke exhorts humanity to be brave enough to "hold to the difficult." It's relatively easy to love when we're feeling grand or to disappear when the going gets rough. What's strenuous is "holding to the difficult": acknowledging one's gruesome past, dreary present, or alien future. "Holding to the difficult" mandates facing another human being with an active gaze and level glance rather than fighting or fleeing.

"Love being difficult" impels us to be tough enough to discipline a child, brave enough to navigate farewells, large enough to enfold society's outcasts. Just when we think our task is done, love insists upon yet one more appropriate demand. Just when we are lured to coast in our marriage, love reminds us that more truthful, trusting communication is wanted. Just when we would rather remain comfortably speciest, love calls us to recognize the souls of animals.

We humans never capture love in its completeness; at best, we merely approximate it in daily exchanges and endeavors. As Truman Capote incisively states:

We are speaking of love...No easy process, understand; it
could take a lifetime, it has mine, and still I've never mas-

tered it—I only know how true it is: that love is a chain of love, as nature is a chain of life.

Eda LeShan tells the story about a dinner party, when she sat next to a woman who was an oceanographer. At one point LeShan was asked if she had ever wondered why lobsters could weigh one pound, three pounds, even ten pounds when they had such a hard shell. How could they grow? Eda had to tell her dinner companion that resolving this fascinating quandary wasn't high on her list of priorities.

The woman smiled and proceeded to explain that when a lobster is crowded in its shell and can't grow anymore, it instinctively travels to some place in the sea, hoping for relative safety and begins to shed its shell. It's a terribly dangerous process—the lobster has to risk its life, because once it becomes naked and vulnerable, it could be dashed against a reef or eaten by another lobster or fish. But that's the only way it can grow.

Plenty of times, my wife and I, singly and as partners, have known that it was time "to go to the reef"—to grow and change, to become more resourceful, more of our best selves. All of us experience nagging discontent with where and who we are that drives us to the reef, since staying in a tight shell spells certain stagnation.

Such is the challenge of the advancing century. To shed our shells, go to the reef, break through self-imposed, constricting barriers, risk enlarging our personal and communal lives, open ourselves to the blessings of loving and being loved: by causes, by humans, by deities, by animals, by life itself!

KEEP THE GIFT MOVING

Beloved, let us love one another; for love is of God,
and they who love are born of God and know God.

I John 4: 7

God wants to be thought of as our Lover.

Julian of Norwich

Love is not to be paid back, it is to be passed on.

Herbert Tarr

E very world religion holds that love is the ascendant principle of a universe into which we were graciously born
and of which we are an integral part. Lest earthlings succumb
to arrogance, we must concede that a Reality beyond our creation, comprehension, and control (be it referenced as God,
Goddess, Creation, Evolution, or Spirit isn't crucial) loved us
into existence. The fundamental nature of Ultimate Mystery
reveals a fount of universal and boundless love, inclusive of
all creatures and infinitely sympathetic.

Our human destiny is to love in reply. We cannot repay Eternal Love, but we can and must respond in kind. As lovers, we
become partners with the divine in healing and sustaining the
cosmos.

In the famous 13th chapter of I Corinthians, Paul places love
at the center of religion and at the heart of life's meaning. He
acknowledges that pious acts, sacrifices, knowledge, proph-
ecy, ecstatic utterance, while important, are but surface mani-
festations of the overruling truth of religion: love. As G. K.
Chesterton noted: "Religion should be more of a love affair
than an abstraction." Deeds not creeds, behavior not belief.

5

Are we loving or not? Loved, do we love in return?

Bishop McConnell, of the Iowa Conference of the Methodist Church, once received a letter from one of his rural congregations which said that they were being subverted by a bunch of Holy Rollers. This group joined the congregation and then brought in a load of hay, threw it on the floor and began to roll around in fits of ecstasy. The congregation was so upset by this apparent folderol that they wanted the Bishop to kick the Holy Rollers out of the church. The Bishop wired back: "All I want to know is this: When they get up from rolling around on the floor, are they better partners? Are they better parents? Are they better citizens? If they are, let me know, and I'll send a bale of hay to every Methodist congregation in the county!"

There are four primary, indivisible destinations for our loving: God, neighbor, self, and the natural world. Life is not a multiple-choice test where we can pick the favored spot for our affection. Healthy loving is expansive not exclusionary; it reaches within, without, and beyond in order to be both fulfilled and fulfilling. We are not permitted to hoard or bask in love's grace but are urged to spread it. The entire creation hankers for and banks upon human loving. As Alice Walker so plainly states: "Service is the rent we pay for being on earth."

Revisiting the ancient Ten Commandments, that 3000-year-old set of moral guidelines, we discern the kernel of responsive loving. The most underrated yet crucial verse in the entire chapter of Exodus isn't any specific commandment but the prologue itself: "And God spoke saying, 'I am the Lord your God, who brought you out of the land of Egypt, out of the house of bondage!'" (Exodus 20:2) Not only are we humans created in love but *saved* by love as well.

The entire Decalogue hinges on the saving event of the Exodus. Because Yahweh has liberated the Israelites from slavery, they are spurred to demonstrate justice and mercy. These ethi-

6

cal imperatives are in direct response to mighty works and precious gifts beyond human doing. Ethics follow the internal and external Exoduses in our existence. We love in response to being set free.

The Ten Commandments, therefore, are not mandates in a vacuum or demands in the desert. Hebraic religion maintains we do genuinely good deeds not out of guilt nor fear, nor out of the wish to impress our neighbors or gain heaven. We conduct moral lives because we know of no better way to say thank you to God, to Life itself—for being created, for being liberated, for being loved ceaselessly. Leading lives of gratitude, we remember the sabbath day, to keep it holy; we honor our fathers and mothers; we refuse to kill, adulterate, or steal from our loves; and we won't bear false witness against or covet the possessions of our neighbors.

When I entered the ministry I was guided, if not driven, by the prompting: "Hey, I've *got* to love." After thirty-plus years in this strange and wondrous profession, I realize that my early inducement was a bit confused and compulsive. I now know that "I *get* to love." Surrounded by the affection of spiritual kin and immersed in divine love dwelling at the heart of Creation, I am pulled by thankfulness, not pushed by approval. I am consequently able to love both intensely and long. Maturing from a vision of "I've got to love" to one of "I get to love" has made an immeasurable difference in my life-journey.

Surely, one of love's gravest opponents is greed. Avarice lies not merely in craving possessions but, moreover, in the act of possessing. Greed begins when we refuse to accept life's gift of love as sufficient and try to acquire more things and money, more ideas and time as well.

We collect resentments. We even stockpile friends. We overdose on our own egos. The only antidote to greed is generosity. Knowing that we are loved from start to finish, and that love is sufficient, we are set free to keep the gift moving, to shower other beings with compassion. We can become magnanimous, literally "great-souled." Indeed, in Buddhist religion, the **bodhisattva** vows not to enter enlightenment until he or she has helped all sentient beings become enlightened.

Love's generosity poses two stern reminders. First, God's love is huge and welcomes into its grasp the marginalized, earth's outcasts. It is tempting to believe that we humans are special in God's eyes, instead of recognizing God's limitless, inclusive gaze. As the poet W. H. Auden warns: "For the error bred in the bone of each woman and each man craves what it cannot have. Not universal love but to be loved alone." Indeed, God's love is distinguished by its all-encompassing embrace. God simply refuses to play favorites. At the final banquet, states the biblical parable, persons from the entire globe—east and west, north and south—will be invited to partake. Undoubtedly, there will be individuals present whom we have shunned and would never have thought to invite.

Second, we can never fully **repay** the creation (craving to earn eternal life on the basis of merits), but we can **respond** to life with love. We can carry our fair share. Love neither starts with nor ends with us, but during the interval we enjoy on earth, we are responsible to personify love.

III

EARTH'S THE RIGHT PLACE

And we are put on earth a little space, that we may
learn to bear the beams of love...

Blake

Earth's the right place for love; I don't know where
it's likely to go better.

Robert Frost

Doug Babcock recounts an enchanting tale about the duck
who has religion:

*Now we are ready to look at something pretty special. It is
a duck riding the ocean a hundred feet beyond the surf. No,
it isn't a seagull. A gull always has a raucous touch about
it. This is some sort of duck who cuddles in the swells. She
isn't cold, and she is thinking things over. There is a big
heaving in the Atlantic Ocean and she is part of it.*

*She looks a bit like a mandarin or the Lord Buddha medi-
tating under the Bo Tree. But she has hardly enough above
the eyes to be a philosopher. She has poise, however, that all
philosophers must have. She can rest while the Atlantic
heaves, because she rests in the Atlantic. Probably she
doesn't know how large the ocean is but, after all, neither
do we. But she realizes it.*

*And what does she do, I ask you? She just sits down in it.
She reposes in the immediate as if it were infinity. That's
religion and the duck has it. She has made herself part of*

*the boundless by easing herself into it just where it touches
her. I like the duck.*

She may not know much, but she's got religion.

Lovers like ducks repose in the immediate as if it were infinity. We become active participants in a relentless encounter with the reality we must face rather than with any realm
we might fancy. Reality like the ocean isn't always pleasant
or comfortable, but lovers refuse to escape this world. We engage it, we sit smack down in it. Authentic love reposes in
every part of earthly existence: in our intelligence, our sexuality, our creativity, our work, our patriotism, our friendships,
our devotional life.

Love never manifests itself in some pure state, separate from
the messy complexities of our actual lives. Love is the sense
and glory we make out of this earthly jaunt. Unquestionably,
the globe contains more beauty and injustice, more joy and
sadness than any one heart can engulf during its single visit.
Yet our souls can stay evergreen, right where we dwell, if we
give ourselves unreservedly to life's flow.

There is much humans can't control, but we can refuse to
renege on our commitments. We can refuse to walk out on
social causes when they become unpopular, refuse to abandon our faith community over a disagreement, refuse to desert
our friends when they are beleaguered, refuse to relinquish
our principles during irksome times. A hard blessing, love
challenges us to stay truthful, stay awake, stay put in our current affectional ties whether at home, at work, at church, at
play or while serving.

May that be our vow upon entering the 21st century: to love
and be loved, for better and for worse, precisely where we're
planted. May we give our all to the relationships in which we
reside rather than being waylaid by daydreams. May we fight
evil on the battlefields we inhabit rather than trying to solve

the problems of a foreign land. As Audre Lorde put it: "We are the ones we've been waiting for," and Thoreau echoes a similar sentiment: "Wherever I sat, there I might live." But unless we take a deep seat right we live and move and have our beings, we will be infernally bedeviled with wanderlust.

Love becomes fraudulent unless demonstrated toward those nigh and dear to us, including family and friends. One of life's tragedies is that people are often more adept at giving love to strangers than kin, dodging the imperative of loving nearby.

Mythologist Joseph Campbell tells a story on this very point. A troubled woman came to the Indian sage Ramakrishna, saying, "O Master, I do not find that I love God." He asked, "Is there nothing, then, that you love?" She responded, "Well, my little nephew." And he said to her, "Therein lies your love and service to God, in your love and service to that child."

Love would pick the rigorous path: assisting others with eye-to-eye caring rather than solely giving through the mail or to external projects. It's usually less dazzling to drive someone to a doctor's appointment or make them a hot meal than to march for civil liberties. Now, don't get me wrong. Both service to the larger world and caring for our friends and neighbors are crucial for full-fledged loving.

It has been said that some activists, when confronted with Jesus on the cross, would probably spend more time producing petitions to halt crucifixions than actually caring for him directly. During our earthly stay, love would demand that we do some of both: petitioning and caregiving. Outreach and inreach, like Siamese twins, cannot be torn asunder.

Yes, earth is the right place for love. Our imperfect, impure love.

It is tempting to turn moral sages like Gandhi into unattainable saints. Deified, Gandhi can always be dismissed as a remote idealist; humanized, his life begs to be studied and his nonviolence to be pursued. Gandhi often reminded his companions that there is nothing he was accomplishing that another person could and should not aspire to accomplish. Gandhi, like Mother Teresa and countless other exemplars, is a thoroughgoingly human, earth-bound creature like ourselves, beset with handicaps and imperfections.

As a partner and parent, Gandhi was definitely foibled. He was married at the age of thirteen to Kasturbai, an unformed teenager as well. Their parents made the match but didn't tell them until wedding preparations were underway. "Two innocent children unwittingly hurled on the ocean of life," with presumably only their experiences in a former incarnation to guide them. Gandhi later decried "the cruel custom of child marriage."

Their marriage was a stormy one, especially in the early years. Many times Mohan and Kasturbai wouldn't even speak to each other. Gandhi experienced moments of extreme jealousy over his wife and was a domineering, sometimes petulant, husband who felt it was his right to impose his will upon her.

Gandhi, in forming his ashram, had insisted on bringing "untouchables" into the household. Kasturbai had accepted this without complaint. She found it too much, however, when her husband required that she assume the job of removing their toilet wastes from the house, something he himself was unwilling to do. As Gandhi later confessed: "I was a cruelly kind husband. I regarded myself as her teacher and so harassed her out of my blind love for her." I'm not sure his love was blind so much as gravely limited and insensitive.

Gandhi was also an incompetent father to his four sons. Expecting them to be junior saints, Gandhi denied them a formal education on the grounds that character was more critical than learning and a profession in public service.

Gandhi's eldest son, in a desperate bid to be free, became everything his father was not: a meat eater, a drinker of alcohol, a gambler, and a convert to Islam. He wound up embezzling money. Gandhi paid the sum back, then printed an account of the affair in his newspaper, *Young India*, concluding that "people may be good, but not necessarily their children."

Regrettably, it was easier for Gandhi to love disciples than his own children, those afar than those nearby. He used to say: "All India is my family." In truth, more his family than his own wife and offspring. This is a tragic yet common plight for public leaders.

Love summons us to care and caress precisely where we're planted on this one, magnificent, earth.

IV
NOBODY BUT YOURSELF

To be nobody but yourself in a world which is doing its best, night and day, to make you everybody else—means to fight the hardest battle which any human being can fight, and never stop fighting.

e. e. cummings

Love is not love, if it forces you to compromise who you are.

Phyllis Chesler

To love oneself is the beginning of a life-long romance.

Oscar Wilde

Till it has loved, no man or woman can become itself.

Emily Dickinson

It would be lamentable to arrive at death's door and realize that we had been solely imitating other people all along the way.

Self-love establishes the cornerstone of the mature life. Our own house must stand in good condition before our being concerned about neighbors or animals or strangers or deities. As Gloria Steinem starkly phrases it: "Self-esteem isn't everything; it's just that there's nothing without it."

Self-regard is our greatest spiritual resource as soul-journeyers. Unless we consistently care about ourselves in invigorating ways, the rest of creation will receive from us a watered-down, idolatrous form of love. Self-neglect, indeed self-abuse, is possibly love's number one enemy. Self-fulfillment is easy to espouse, but confounding to practice. Authentic self-love is a lifelong struggle, an uphill battle. There are internal and social forces, even religious practices, militating against our finding, then fulfilling, our true beings. We cannot have a sound society until we have enough self-assured women and men who cannot be bought—what might be called unpurchasable individuals. There is the story of William Shawn, the superb *New Yorker* editor, about whom it was said: "He held to the resolve never to publish anything or have something written for a hidden reason: to pander to somebody, to build up or tear somebody down, to indulge a personal friendship or animosity, or to propagandize. Everything published in the *New Yorker* was precisely what it purported to be, published for its own sake." Now, there was an unpurchasable individual!

When Yahweh in the Old Testament was pressed to describe himself, his most vivid description was simply: "**I am who I am**." Beneath all our accomplishments and aspirations lies our basic identity. Mirroring the Creator, we creatures are who we are. Integrity has to do with our being integrated, undivided and complete, whole persons. As Judy Garland reminds us: "Always be a first-rate version of yourself instead of a second-rate version of somebody else."

Self-care is holistic: requiring that we nourish, on a daily basis, the entirety of our beings—spirit, mind, body, heart, and conscience. Lovers replenish the spirit through silent retreat, refuel the mind through continuing education, recreate the body through exercise and nutrition, renew the heart through support groups and professional counseling, and restore the conscience through justice-building and peace-making.

Self-pity is one of the most popular, non-pharmaceutical drugs in our society. Self-pity is narcotic because its gives momentary pleasure and separates us from actuality. It impels us to cry out: "The situation is hopeless; poor me, there's nothing I can do!" Then it becomes all right to do absolutely nothing but wallow in misery. Yet no matter how the fates conspire, we still make or forsake our own destinies.

Self-pitying sorts are forever wishing they were someone else who had more smarts or money or looks. It is warped self-esteem run amok. As Allan Gurganus describes: "On life's totem pole of bargain basement emotions, jealousy and self-pity are the tackiest." Jesus didn't stand for self-pitying sorts. He was known to have said to more than one slacker: "Rise, take up your pallet and walk."

As lovers we are called to pursue self-renewal rather than get derailed by self-pity, to deal directly with the disappointments we face, to make the best of the rough situations in which we find ourselves. It is love's difficult lesson to whistle rather than whine when walking home in the dark.

I relish the story about the woman in Budapest who goes to her rabbi and complains, "Life is unbearable. There are nine of us living in one room. What can I do?" The rabbi answers, "Take your goat into the room with you." The woman is incredulous, but the rabbi insists. "Do as I say and come back in a week."

A week later the woman returns looking more distraught than ever. "We can't stand it," she tells the rabbi. "The goat is filthy." The rabbi then tells her, "Go home and let the goat out. And come back in a week." A radiant woman returns to the rabbi a week later, exclaiming, "Life is beautiful. We enjoy every minute of it now that there's no goat...only the nine of us." Modest shifts in the environment can prove transformative to one's attitude!

A word of caution concerning self-esteem. We negotiate a fine line between mature self-love and narcissism or what Martin Luther termed *incurvatum in se*, meaning "turned in upon oneself." It is all right to stare at our navels, if when we do so, we acknowledge our vital connection to other people. We are not sufficient unto ourselves. It is only in the context of community that we become fully human. We are *embedduals* (Robert Kegan's phrase): "Individuals embedded in communities of meaning." When the apostle Paul observed that we "are members one of another," he used the word *member* in its original sense of limb. For we are truly one another's arms and legs at times. Lacking one another, we are incomplete, maimed, less than human.

V

A POLICY, NOT AN EMOTION

If I were fire, I would burn; if I were a woodcutter, I would strike; but I am a heart and I love!
Nikos Kazantzakis

Love is or it ain't. Thin love ain't love at all.
Toni Morrison

If Rosa Parks had taken a poll before she sat down in the bus in Montgomery, she'd still be standing.
Mary Frances Berry

One of life's hard learnings, oft-forgotten, is that love is primarily an activity not a feeling, a verb rather than a noun. Or as Hugh Bishop phrases it: "Love is not an emotion; it's a policy!" Sentiments come cheaply; actions cost. In truth, love comprises a series of activities, not an isolated deed.

Love extracts a steep but reasonable price. We love knowing full well that we will lose one another someday. Every love relationship ends in a loss—death or dissolution; therefore, love's very impermanence makes it imperative that we hold one another tightly yet freely during this mortal dance. As James Baldwin echoed: "The moment we fail to hold one another, the sea engulfs us and the light goes out." Note he mentions **hold**, not cling to, one another.

The hype in modern mass media claims that we should be able to fall in and out of love rather felicitously. If only we wear the proper deodorant or name-brand clothes, if only we discard a few moral inhibitions, if only we surround ourselves with certain glamorous folk, then sexual and emotional power, love itself, will be ours for the taking.

We women and men too often pursue second-and-third-rate versions of real love...coasting without commitment or gravitating to love-substitutes. We confuse addictive for passionate behavior. We run from love because of fear, because we have been burned, because the cost appears too high, or because we are just plain stuck on ourselves.

As a minister I have spoken directly on the subject of love but rarely. Not because I underestimate love's value. Hardly. Love is of critical importance. But *talking* about love doesn't get us to the real article. Preaching about love can, in fact, be a poor alternative for being or doing love where it both counts and costs, in our daily lives. Life's central vow is loving and being loved. All else is footnote.

Idries Shah, the renowned Sufi scholar, once told an audience after lecturing a full four hours: "Notice I didn't use the actual words God or Love once during my talk, yet everything I mentioned was somehow about these two realities."

In keeping with Shah's sentiment, we must primarily practice what we periodically preach. Love means labor. We hear a lot of people say that love is basically natural. Let it flow, let it be. If we have to work at love, they say, then it isn't worth it. Love will surely have its smooth moments. But over the long haul, we need to be intentional about cultivating love. Love is an art, and like other arts, it requires supreme discipline, concentration, patience, concern, and practice. Love has little to do with staying comfortable and doing convenient things. Loving costs.

When we don't like certain things about our country, our relationships, or our work, love would encourage us not to drop out or run away but to stick around and try to change the conditions. Love asks us not to burn the flag but to wash it. As Barbara Kingsolver so deftly puts it:

A country can be flawed as a marriage or family or person is flawed, but 'love it or leave it' is a coward's slogan. There's more honor in 'love it and get it right. Love it, love it and never shut up.'

Love knows that friendships and partnerships are not made in heaven but shaped on earth, and they need all the mindfulness we can muster. Love withers from malnutrition.

Regrettably, too much of American romance is tunnel-visioned, secretive. In the early years of my ministry, the 1970's to be precise, countless couples trekked off to the ocean or hills to get married, preferably without the benefit of clergy, even the presence of friends. They might do this on a Saturday, then unexpectedly appear at my office on Monday and ask me to play functionary by signing their legal document. In my wiser moments I would refuse their request, not only because it seemed demeaning to my profession but also because it diminished the scope of the love-partnership as I saw it.

I have always believed that neither I nor the state nor the church marries couples. I officiate at the ceremony, but they wed one another. Nonetheless, there are reasons for making a private partnership a public event. There are reasons for having friends and religious leadership present. The main reason is not born of law or society, duty or pressure. It is born of love.

Love claims that no two people finally live unto themselves. They dwell in the larger family of humankind. It takes a whole village to raise one committed couple. Therefore, during every ceremony I draw a pledge from the gathered congregation that they dedicate themselves "to the continuing task of helping Ellen and Gary build a deep and abiding love." Ellen and Gary are interwoven with and indebted to those friends they already know and those they have yet to meet, and this fact must be acknowledged continually.

In its original sense, "idiot" signified a purely private, narcissistic person. John Stuart Mill was right on target when he declared marriage to be "a primary political experience." A couple's affection for one another must motivate and strengthen them to love the world beyond their nest. Hence, when we trust or forgive our partner, we don't halt there, we are learning how to trust or forgive others outside our principal love-bond. The point of joining lives is to gain spheres of accountability and blessing beyond our imagining and our satisfied souls. To be otherwise would be idiotic.

VI
TWIN ARTS

Love cures people, both the ones who give it and
the ones who receive it.

Karl Menninger

Impart as much as you can of your spiritual being
to those who are on the road with you. And accept
as something precious what comes back to you from
them.

Albert Schweitzer

L ove's hard blessing would call us to move ambidextrously
between the active and passive voices, or as progressive
20th-century African-American minister Howard Thurman
urged: "My heart must be a swinging door that opens in and
opens out." We lovers need to allow others into our hearts,
encouraging them to caress us, even carry us upon occasion.
For life's central vow is loving *and* being loved.

Good givers are good receivers as well. Some people say it
is more blessed to give than to receive, taking their cue from
the biblical injunction. Others say it is more blessed to receive
than to give, taking their lead from society's egotism. Love
says what is actually blessed is that when we receive, to accept joyously and thankfully **and** when we give, to offer gen-
erously and creatively.

Lovers practice the twin arts of giving and receiving. For if
we aren't receiving bountifully, our giving turns martyrish.
And if we aren't giving responsibly, our receiving becomes
exploitative. Torn in two, they produce lopsided loving.

Some among us have trouble receiving from the abundance
of life. We refuse unearned gifts, contending that what we

don't merit isn't ours to have. Or we only feel comfortable receiving if we have a chance to return the favor. Or we are self-satisfied. Whatever the reason, some of us never quite learn how to receive with any sense of grace or gratitude.

Several years ago, I was idly strumming my guitar and crooning away at a church camp when someone remarked: "You really have a lovely voice." I had never heard that accolade before or, at least, it hadn't fully registered. More to the point, I wasn't at all sure that it was true. So I deflected the gift with rationalizations and "Yes, buts!"— responding with everything but a plain "thank you." A friend sitting near me was bothered by my show of false modesty and blurted out: "Come on, Tom, just receive the gift, just say Thanks." Reluctantly I did, and ever since that awkward exchange, I have been more comfortable in receiving compliments about my singing voice.

The legend goes that the devil once went for a walk with a friend. They saw a woman ahead of them stoop down and pick up something from the road.

"What did that woman find?" asked the friend.

"A piece of truth," said the devil.

"Doesn't that disturb you?" asked the friend.

"No, it does not," said the devil, "I shall allow her to make a belief out of it."

Sadly, religious folks, along with lovers, are prone to make rigid systems out of partial wisdoms picked up along the road. Giving is such a half-truth, and so is receiving. Both are required in rhythmic measure to fashion wholistic loving.

Responsive recipients are invariably contented givers, for these two lost arts are not different in kind. Practiced in tandem, we are infused with love. When we receive something with genuine enthusiasm, we exude warmth, we send forth appreciation; we are, in effect, giving of ourselves. The converse is equally valid. When our giving is unqualified, we bring something home to our heart, we receive.

VII
THY NEIGHBOR AS THYSELF

The love of our neighbor, in all its fullness, simply means being able to say 'What are you going through?'

Simone Weil

What matters is love. So just practice loving. Love a Russian. You'd be surprised how easy it is and how it will brighten your morning. Love an Iranian, a Vietnamese, people not just here but everywhere. Then when you've gotten really good at it, try something hard like loving the politicians in our nation's capital.

George Wald

Love Thy Neighbor as Thyself: these paired commandments from both the Old and New Testaments are effortless to utter, yet difficult to execute. Loving God is sometimes smoother than either loving yourself or others, because God can remain conveniently remote, whereas humans are vexingly in one another's faces. Again, as Rilke reminds us:

For one human being to love another, that is perhaps the most difficult of all our tasks, the ultimate, the last test and proof, the work for which all other work is but preparation.

Love thy neighbor AS thyself means: "as much as" "not more or less than." There is an implied equal sign in this sentence. In short, you can't love your neighbor without enjoying yourself.

We may idolize our neighbors, be infatuated or symbiotic with them, but we cannot truly care about others without having a similar density and depth of respect for ourselves. Those who have succumbed to either egocentricity or self-loathing remain stuck on feeble, shaky images of themselves, whereas sufficient self-caring impels us to nourish earth and neighbor with tenderness.

Another way to put it is: if we don't love ourselves, then we don't have much of worth and substance to grant others. We can't give away what we don't possess in ample measure ourselves!

But who is my neighbor? In recent times we have evolved a cosmic consciousness that expands the concept of neighbor to include not only friends and acquaintances but strangers and foreigners, even non-human life. Love is getting more difficult as its embrace broadens.

Being a valued neighbor is a complicated enterprise: What works at one time and place is seldom reproducible for the next encounter. Bernard Cooke was accurate: "Involvement with people is always a very delicate thing; it requires real maturity to become involved and not get all messed up."

We start by recognizing that our mission as a good neighbor is to be a supporter more than a helper. Supporters challenge others to remain accountable for handling their own problems. Helpers try to do for others what they are capable of doing for themselves. Supporters are willing to give information; helpers try to give advice, even when unasked.

To become supporters rather than rescuers, we need to practice what Buddha espoused: "Don't just do something, stand there!" Be available, care by being present. Stand still, strong, alongside. Being empathic means being sensitive enough to the climb into the pit with another, while retaining enough resilience to be able to make the trip back out. For if we both go under, all is lost. Brandy Lovely aptly phrases the dilemma:

We all know misery loves company, but if everyone joins the misery, then who will relieve the situation? Compassion is the faculty by which we acknowledge another's agony, without joining it.

Finally, the law of boundaries must be respected. Jesus was a realist about this. He didn't propose absolute concern for the welfare of others. He included a limit. When he uttered the first part of the great commandment about loving God, it was unconditional: "Thou shalt love the Lord thy God with all thy heart, and with all thy soul, and with all thy mind!"

But when he spoke of loving thy neighbor, the word "all" was not used. Instead, he said, "as thyself." This indicates a limit to how much we love our neighbor. The qualification, "as thyself" implies that the survival of self is the limit of one's love for one's neighbor. Consequently, to be effective in loving others we have to preserve our own strength and integrity. A good neighbor doesn't burn out or play martyr.

The law of boundaries is abrogated at great expense. In terms of evolution, those plants and animals that selectively limited their growth-boundaries survived, while the dinosaurs perished through excessive development. The same principle applies in human intercourse. Our responses to the needs of our neighbors must be discriminating, lest we become overwhelmed.

Love thy neighbor *as* thyself. We can act in a neighborly love only to the extent that we preserve our integrity by loving ourselves. If we respect our boundaries, we can conserve our stamina to help others in the priority of our relationships. And our neighboring will prove effective yet resilient.

VIII
EVERY GRAIN OF SAND

For thou shalt be in league with the stones of the field, and the beasts of the field shall be at peace with thee.

Job 5:23

Love all God's creation, the whole of it and every grain of sand. Love every leaf and every ray of God's light. Love the animals, love the plants, love everything. If you love everything you will perceive the divine mystery in things.

Fyodor Dostoevsky

I was in love with the whole world and all that lived in its rainy arms.

Louise Erdrich

Another formidable lesson of love exhorts us to bring not only all races and nations but other species within our moral circle of concern, consciousness, and connectedness.

Animals are not lower than humans, only different. We share earth's home. Native Americans conduct a ritual called "the making of relatives," where they pledge to adopt all living entities as kith and kin, related yet separate wonders of a unified creation.

We two-legged lovers are summoned to *behold*. Behold the lilies of the field. Behold the moon. Behold the raccoon. Behold the sunset. Behold even the tornado, for we cannot wrest beauty from the whole. Everywhere we roam in the universe we find loveliness mingled with the harsh and disturbing. And behold the rocks, for a brook without rocks has no song. As naturalist William Barrett recalls:

> *The rocks are no less individuals. Whoever thinks matter is mere inert stuff has not looked long at rocks. They do not lie inert, they thrust forward, or crouch back in quiet self-gathered power. The living rock. More than an idle phrase. Out of the living rock the waters of spirit.*

Beyond affirming our **relatedness** to the entire ecosystem, beyond displaying **respect** for all living things, there is the undeniable charge for lovers to be **responsible**.

In the Garden of Eden myth, we were given the imperative to tend it, "to till and keep it," to be caretakers. Life itself was deeded to human beings under the requirement that we remain obedient to its basic laws and prove responsible for creation's well-being. And tilling means more than having a green thumb. Some of us don't own green thumbs, and we're hardly exempt from the caretaking of earth.

I used to plant gardens in Iowa, a land with as lush, fertile ground as exists anywhere in America. I learned always to keep the empty seed packages. Sometimes they were just the right size for storing my crop! Tilling means cultivating an evergreen spirit. We must be stewards even if not planters.

Consequently, we are summoned to use the simple tools at our disposal as loving humans—all the tools needed to till and tend earth's elements. The tools of technology, the tools of economics, the tools of politics, and especially the tools of the religious spirit—a spirit born in wonder, filled with gratitude, sparked by relatedness, respect, and responsibility. A spirit awash with love, for we cannot sustain that which we do not revere.

Each act of compassion for the natural world, each measure of conservation, each decision against dirtying the air, land or water—these are gifts of the highest order, gifts back to the Divine Love that brought us into being and will not let us go. We cannot do the perfect thing; we can only approximate deeds that are helpful not harmful in each situation.

There is unity in the ecosphere within which we exist in quivering ambivalence. We are unable to comprehend fully the whole and all its precarious rhythms and equities in the very moment in which we are required to act. We simply respond with exceeding care and tenderness. We ask and answer with our lives: "What can the planet best do through me at this particular juncture of my earthly stay?"

In these late years of our planet's need, we will most likely never halt either our intentional plundering or our accidental blundering, even the most loving among us. Our spaceship is fragile and frail. And so are we, its stewards. We remain defined more by our aspirations than by our achievements.

As loving folk we aspire to heed the words of the Sioux holy leader Black Elk who said:

> *The earth is sacred and is a relative of ours and this we should remember when we call her Grandmother or Mother. We are related to all things: the earth and the stars, everything, and with all these together, we raise our hands to the Great Spirit.*

IX

LIE BACK
AND THE SEA WILL HOLD YOU

Lie back daughter, let your head be tipped back in the cup of my hand, gently, and I will hold you. Spread your arms wide, lie out on the stream and look high at the gulls. A dead person's float is face down. You will dive and swim soon enough, for this tide water ebbs to the sea. Daughter, believe me. When you tire on the long thrash to your island, lie up and survive. And as you float now, where I held you and let go, remember, when fear cramps your heart, what I told you. Lie gently and wide to the light-year stars. Lie back and the sea will hold you.

Philip Booth

When Mrs. Albert Einstein was asked if she understood her husband's Theory of Relativity, she replied, "No...But I know my husband and he can be trusted!"

W hen I was a young boy of ten, I started the first of several paper routes. I was taught a memorable lesson by an older woman who lived alone on my route. Increasingly blind, Mrs. Thorne came to the place where she could no longer see to make proper change when paying her monthly bill for the paper. One Saturday morning, when I went collecting, Mrs. Thorne drew her old leather pocketbook, with a snap on top, from her pocket, handed it to me and said, "Tom, I can't see any more; please help yourself to what I owe you!" As I opened the purse, I was suddenly struck with what a wonderful thing it was to be trusted!

Trust is our core perception, our way of seeing and sizing

up the world. The trusting person claims that it is right and good to be alive. Trust gambles that the universe is essentially benign. Trust is the confidence that we humans can survive our fumbling intellect, contorted affections, perpetual slips without falling prey to despair. The trusting person can blurt out: "I am surrounded and sustained by support even when I seem to be sinking." In short, trusters dare to "lie gently and wide to the light-year stars."

When I trust my own inner processes, I am able to become the person I am meant to become. When I trust you, I am able to allow you to share life's journey with me. I am able to love. Trust is essential to a stable, enduring devotional bond, be it between family members, partners, or work associates.

One psychologist concludes that there are essentially two core emotions—fear and trust, and we can choose which emotion will predominate in any given moment. Trust enriches our experience; fear robs it. Furthermore, high trusters are themselves more trustworthy. Mature lovers are trusting and trustworthy people.

To trust is to be related to someone in such a way that our heart is invested and our hope focused. Trust is what makes possible the fragile merger of freedom and commitment in any viable relationship. Without trust, the commitment is worthless. With trust, each of us can allow the other acceptable freedom. Loving is neither a passive enterprise nor a one-way matter. Sometimes I evoke trust from you. Sometimes you initiate it in me. But when our relationship is thriving, trust flows back and forth, and we are both dynamic agents. We can resonate to Sam Keen's sentiment: "Trust is the most powerful aphrodisiac available to us humans."

To trust someone does not require certitude. While adequate evidence must be present, there is never final proof. We cannot conclusively justify our trustworthiness to anyone, even our loved ones. If we could, we would be referring to something other than trust.

Trust, then, is a union of some data, some gamble, some buoyancy, some grace, some release. In matters of partnering and parenting, politics and religion, where trust is sorely tested, the depth and power of our love is in direct proportion to the fountain of our trust.

One of the books on the mandatory reading list during my 1960's seminary training was the *Autobiography of Malcolm X*, as assisted by Alex Haley, author of *Roots*. This memoir retells the absorbing story of an African-American man who rose from being a hoodlum, thief, dope peddler, and pimp to become indispensable leader of the Black Revolution. If anyone made a remarkable comeback from mistrust and distrust it was Malcolm X.

He had to grow trust from scratch as an adult even between himself and members of his own race—evidenced in the years of collaboration between Malcolm X and Alex Haley in the writing of this book. Their relationship ripens in trust until, as Haley reports in the epilogue:

> When Malcolm made long trips, such as to San Francisco and Los Angeles, I did not go along, but frequently, usually very late at night, he would telephone me, and ask how the book was coming along, and he might set up the time for our next interview upon his return.
>
> One call that I never will forget came at close to 4 a.m., waking me; he must have just gotten up in Los Angeles. His voice said: 'Alex Haley?' I said, sleepily, 'Yes? Oh, hey, Malcolm!' His voice said, 'I trust you seventy per cent!' and then he hung up.
>
> I lay a short time thinking about him, and I went back to sleep feeling warmed by that call, as I am still warmed to remember it. Neither of us ever mentioned it.

Trust is superfluous if we claim the final answers to living and dying, or if we avoid deep friendship or loving while on earth. But at least 70% trust is essential to those of us who, like Alex Haley and Malcolm X, choose the route of creative insecurity, of freedom-within-faithfulness.

X

GOD IN THE LURKING-PLACES

You can't tame God, who's wild, you know.
                                              C. S. Lewis

Let God alone if need be. Methinks, if I loved him
more, I should keep him, I should keep myself rather,
at a more respectful distance. It is not when I am
going to meet God, but when I am just turning away
and leaving God alone, that I discover that God is. I
say, God. I am not sure that that is the name.
                                       Henry David Thoreau

The purpose of the loving life is to maintain an honest, current, deepening encounter with self, neighbor, nature, and God. Since deity resides beyond human comprehension or control, any notes we humans chance about the divine say more about us—our quirks and our evolution—than about Ultimacy.

Lovers are disinterested in debating the existence of God or nit-picking about the nature of God but willingly point toward some of the hide-outs, what Thoreau called the "lurking-places," of God. Although Thoreau was a devout panentheist, who believed that God was discoverable amidst living realities and inanimate objects, he still maintained reserve in expounding about the Eternal.

Such verbal modesty about God appeals to me more than the oily chumminess with which devotees habitually relate to divine mystery. The Great Spirit will surely not be manipulated by sanctimonious, self-serving petitions. The Creator refuses to be confined to bumper stickers and lampshade slogans.

The most persuasive truth about God is simply that God is not us. God doesn't pander to human wishes but more often than not rattles our foundations by showing up in astonishing, unanticipated places. The fierce paradox obtains: When religious pilgrims don't pressure, even pursue God, when we let God alone, the divine presence may (no firm predictions) pay a surprise visit. Ironically, one so intimate with Yahweh as Moses "went up on Sinai, waited still in a cleft of the rock and saw the backparts of God." (Exodus 33: 22-23)

It is tempting to focus upon the traditional haunts of God such as nature-inspired wonder, sexual ecstasy, musical epiphanies, all of which encounters with the divine may prove both real and becoming, but are reported all too regularly. Here are four lurking-places where I am currently surprised by running into some part, front or back, of the Creator.

Strangers

The first lurking-place of the divine occurs when I greet the diverse strangers along my path. Written on the walls of a Spanish harbor is the aphorism: "I am seeking God, but I do not find God. I am seeking myself, but I do not find me. But I do find my neighbor and the three of us get on our way together." In every religion, hospitality to the stranger constitutes the highest expression of faith, and, in fact, the divine often appears cloaked in the guise of the vagabond, the startling guest, yea, the unlovable.

Stuff

Another unconventional venue for the presence of the Holy lies amid the inanimate matter of the world. Emerson reminds us that "God does not speak prose, but communicates with us by hints, omens, inferences, and dark resemblances in objects around us." Vincent Van Gogh volunteers a matching sentiment: "The best way to know God is to love many things." Note he didn't just say to love many people or projects or landscapes. Rather he said, "to love many things." Van Gogh perceived that the ordinary stuff of our lives is hallowed and furnishes us with a window to the divine. As Zen Buddhism announces: "Pots and pans are the Buddha's body."

Squandering

Humans often lead narrow, prudish lives because we mistakenly believe self-abnegation might bring us closer to God. Not so, according to Jesus, who recounts the story of "a woman who came with an alabaster jar of ointment, very costly, and she broke the jar and poured it over Jesus' head." (Mark 14: 3)

The Nazarene was moved by this spontaneous display of generosity. Indeed, Jesus was always affected by a magnanimous heart. Remember both the centurion exhibiting great faith and the widow placing her entire earnings into the treasury. And now a woman breaks open a very expensive bottle of perfume and lavishes Jesus with it. While the onlookers were dismayed by this prodigal outpouring, Jesus considered it to be **holy** waste. "She has done a beautiful thing to me."

John Mason Brown echoes the same notion when he writes:

> *Existence is a strange bargain. Life owes us little; we owe it everything. The only true happiness comes from squandering ourselves for a purpose.*

Extravagance not niggardliness is a promising avenue to the Eternal One.

Struggle

The story of Jacob wrestling with a being greater than himself in the Old Testament is a paradigm for disclosing Yahweh in the throes of strife. After a tumultuous night of unrelieved struggle, Jacob emerged with a limp and a new name, *Israel*: "the one who strives or struggles with God." Thus, Israel, throughout its spiritual evolution as a nation, comes to represent those people who are willing to rage and wrestle openly with rather than grovel before God. The Jewish religion has always agreed with Carl Sandburg that "God gets tired of too many hallelujahs!"

We struggle with evil. We struggle against injustice. We struggle to be caring parents and devoted partners. We struggle to be good professionals. We struggle to be responsible citizens of the state and compassionate children of the universe. We struggle to love and be loved. Precisely as we struggle, and struggle relentlessly, God is not far off.

XI
PAYING ATTENTION

Where your treasure is, there will your heart be also.
Jesus

My occupation is love. It's all I do.
St. John of the Cross

Most of us are trained to love in bursts but falter over the long haul. While the juices flow and enthusiasm blazes, we love passionately. But love demands more continuity. It would have us attend during the lulls of our journey.

"Attention, attention, attention," wrote Zen Master Ikkyu centuries ago when asked to write down the highest wisdom. "But what does attention mean?" pressed his questioner. Master Ikkyu replied, "Attention means attention." The etymology of **attention** stems from the Latin *attendere*, meaning to "stretch." One way or another, for good or ill, in authentic loving our souls are stretched. Our hearts and minds and bodies as well. As the poet Marge Piercy observes: "Loving leaves stretch marks."

Loving reveres the underrated virtues of hardiness and durability. While taking the vow of stability, lovers are flexible and resilient, bendable as bamboo in the storm rather than stiff trees that fall victim to obsessive control. Lovers remain at our affectional posts, especially during the inevitable seasons of upheaval and bleakness.

Wolfgang Konisburg, also known as Woody Allen, has perceptively mused: "50% of life is showing up!" It certainly takes courage just to roust oneself from the clutches of laziness, to appear when and where we are needed—in relationships, at work stations, for benevolent causes.

But I am equally concerned about the other 50% of life's equation. Attendance isn't adequate to satisfy love's difficult lesson. Once we've arrived, do we pay attention, do we speak truth in love, and then are we willing to surrender the outcomes? Love would have us show up, then give ourselves over, without giving ourselves away, to the unfolding drama.

We cannot love without being fully present and accounted for. The poetic refrain of e. e. cummings teases the world's floaters: "hey, I hear there's a hell of a universe next door, let's go!" But there's a hell of a universe right here as well, a universe not to be spurned. In Sanskrit the word for "concentration" is **samadhi** and refers to "one-pointedness." Whether meditating upon what we cherish or marching for what we prize, lovers are summoned to singleness of focus. Lovers stay on purpose, pay attention, stand liable for what we do with who we are in the chosen bonds of life's journey.

The genesis of Valentine's Day is acutely relevant to the challenge of remaining faithful to the concerns of intimacy, friendship, and social justice.

Valentine was a Roman who was martyred on February 14, AD 270. He wrote a farewell note to the jailer's daughter who had befriended him while he was in prison, signing it: "Your Valentine." Perhaps Valentine's Day should mark that holiday when we not only share notes of affection with our loved ones but also consider the plight of unknown persons incarcerated in the prison system. It is the time to address both individuals and reform institutions. It is the season when we remember that love demands our undivided attention! As Alice Walker notes: "Human compassion is equal to human cruelty and it is up to each of us to tip the balance." Our ounces of love matter.

Valentine's Day is an appropriate celebration to transcend the highly carnal and cotton-candied versions of romance rampant in contemporary culture. Valentine himself would exhort us to pay homage to the demands and disciplines of more expansive loving.

At the close of our earthly treks, there is perhaps no more blessed way to sign our farewell note than with the honorable phrase, Your Valentine!

XII

SHOWING ANGER...EVEN HATE

A wild patience has taken me this far...anger and
tenderness: my selves. And now I believe they breathe
in me as angels, not polarities. Anger and tenderness, the spider's genius to spin and weave in the
same action from her own body, anywhere—even
from a broken web.

Adrienne Rich

When we eat together, as friends, there's always some
music and laughter and there's usually an argument.
There's no desire to argue, it's just the fears and
ferocities that accompany the tunes and poems and
our love. Anything venomous that occurs is fed to
the dogs afterwards.

Michael Meade

Hate has a lot in common with love, chiefly with that
self-transcending aspect of love, the fixation on others, the dependence on them and in fact the delega-
tion of a piece of one's own identity to them...The
hater longs for the object of their hatred.

Vaclav Havel

Anger is one of the most loving emotions we ever
experience. We get angry with those who matter most
to us. Apathy, not anger, is the opposite of love. Anger means
that I care enough to give you the best of myself, including
my underbelly. If we don't care about someone, we don't risk
strong, even negative feelings. Anger-with-heart puts fire into
an alliance: a fire that burns, cleanses, destroys, and heals in
service of relational well-being.

Anger alerts us to the fact that something is missing or gone awry in our companionship. Anger is warmth and aliveness. It produces affective and effective messages. It draws boundaries and creates space within our intimate bonds. Anger signals one of love's difficult lessons—namely, an honest relationship is never only sweetness and light.

We children grow up with rare displays of constructive outrage modeled by the adults in our world. Therefore, we come to believe a batch of unhelpful platitudes like: "If you display anger, then you don't love me," or "Tame your rage, then convert it into a quick and huge smile," or "If you have to get mad, then at least do it politely."

On the contrary, feeling angry is a human phenomenon as universal as feeling hungry or fatigued, lonely or happy. The situations that make humans angry, the ways we grow furious, and the things we do when we are incensed are not the same. Some who are angry would **break** a pot, others will **make** a pot. It all depends.

Lamentably, we fall prey to the harmful extremes of slow-burning bitterness or all-consuming fury. Suppressed anger in a loving relationship can result in insomnia, high blood pressure, fatigue, habitual sarcasm, gastro-intestinal disorders, headaches. Verbal or physical outbursts of anger are also destructive to relational health, either alienating one's partner or escalating a normal conflict into all-out strife.

The challenge for lovers is releasing our anger for impact rather than venting our hostility for injury. There are no pat formulas or simple solutions but a handful of measures are in order.

First, lovers recognize that we are angry. If we are tense or dejected, we inquire: What is bothering me? At whom am I harboring upset? We never need to justify anger. Feelings are facts. Getting angry is neither right nor wrong; it just is.

Second, lovers identify the source of the anger. To deal with our ire, we must locate the real cause, internal or external or a blend of the two, then have the courage to release our anger on target.

Third, we need to cope with our anger realistically. This calls us to deal with small irritations by discussing them openly before they accumulate and produce painful division. There's wisdom in the biblical injunction that lovers not let the sun go down on our anger.

Fourth, we need to establish agreeable rituals for handling anger. Whenever one person I know feels fury bubbling up inside, she lets her beloved know that she has to discharge some rage from her system. He agrees that she can let loose with a verbal tirade, usually for a few minutes. The anger is released with his non-defensive support, so it is less likely to do any damage. Once the heat is off, the two set a future time to talk through the issue.

Another insight. Just as it takes two to tango, so it takes two to tangle. Whether you or your companion are the aggressor, any legitimate conflict belongs to the two of you. It is tempting to scapegoat; "love being difficult" awakens us to the truth that fights can only be resolved when we both realize our culpability and labor to bridge the gulf.

In sum, the pain of conflict signals the price of tender, growing intimacy. It is possible to express anger without attacking the other person's ego. Not easy to be sure, but easy is merely another name for withdrawal, revenge, or compliance. Those who are angry stick close enough to solve arguments and celebrate love. They find ways to be angry together!

HATRED

Let's up the ante. Love must contain anger, but does it entail hatred as well? Naturally, to create a just and beautiful world, evil must be combated and injustice must be loathed. Nonetheless, as William Sloane Coffin cautioned: "We hate the evil only because we so love the good. We must love the good more than we hate the evil, lest we end up being just a good hater."

Additionally, loving persons walk that precarious tight-rope between hating what our enemy does and respecting their humanity with certain inalienable rights. To complicate matters, we invariably hate in others those things we despise in ourselves, since hatred often betrays an underlying self-contempt. Hatred in this sense can be a barrier to self-acceptance.

Someone has noted, "Hatred is a normal neurosis," and Ecclesiastes declared: "There is a time to love and there is a time to hate." However, we must use hate judiciously, lest it devour the hater and destroy the target. What seems prudent is to love boldly **and** hate mindfully. I agree with Olive Moore who wrote:

> *Be careful with hatred. Handle hatred with respect. Hatred is too noble an emotion to be frittered away in little personal animosities. Whereas love is of itself a reward and an object worth striving for, personal hatred has no triumphs that are not trivial, secondary, and human. Therefore love as foolishly as you may. But hate only after long and ardent deliberation. Hatred is a passion requiring one hundred times the energy of love. Keep it for a cause, not an individual, keep it for intolerance, injustice, stupidity. For hatred is the strength of the sensitive. Its power and its greatness depend on the selflessness of its use.*

So it goes. May we employ our hatred not to demolish but to cleanse, not for revenge but for results. Hatred, when discreetly used can be a way of resisting personal wrong or social terror, of drawing limits when human dignity is threatened.

There is a time to hate, but then a time to release from the hatred, and move toward truce. As the *Dhammapada*, the sacred Buddhist scripture, reminds us: "Hatred never ceases by hatred, but by love alone is healed. This is an ancient and eternal law."

XIII

WIDENING CIRCLES

God is always revising our boundaries outward.
Douglas Steere

If there is a fatal notion on this earth, it's the notion
that wider notions will be fatal.
Barbara Kingsolver

To love our own country is splendid, but why should
love stop at the border?
Pablo Casals

I live my life in widening circles that reach out across
the world. I may not ever complete the last one, but
I give myself to it.
Rainer Maria Rilke

The old hymn reminds us that "there's a wideness in God's
mercy," arms engulfing those who live on the outskirts
of human favor, especially the foreigner and the pariah. Being created in God's image, we possess the capacity and charge
to love broadly as well.

Love would not have us ask people what they believe or
what might be their political preference or sexual orientation,
but rather ask their name and how they are doing, really doing. Love bids us to greet one another along life's pathway as
the Quakers of old did: "How goes it with thy spirit?"

As our loving grasp extends, a marvel occurs: The supply
of love is replenished, we are personally refueled. Active loving, then, is a form of transcendence. It widens our horizons
and stretches our beings. Our world is remade. Lovers are not

only interesting to themselves; everything and everyone become more interesting to them.

A poetic expression of love as transcendent is penned by Antoine de Saint Exupéry:

> *Love does not consist in gazing at each other but in looking outward together in the same direction.*

Yet St. Exupéry's lesson of love proves rugged, because it is comforting to stick within the snug confines of our own intimacy. That's exactly what most lovers settle for.

In pre-marital counseling, couples sometimes bask in little more than passional juices. They gushingly swear of their mutual love, but seldom have plumbed its subtle, deeper blessings. My job is to assist them in doing so. I probe with questions like these: "Love's a nice and necessary start, but tell me more. What do you appreciate in particular about your partner? What do you like to do apart from one another? How would you describe your mission in life? What do you fight about? What interests and values do you hold in common? What are your growing edges? How are each of you giving back to society as a result of your declared love for each other?" In co-answering such hard questions, their ardor is able to thicken. Surely, one of the hallmarks of a hearty partnership is the capacity to keep widening its orb of love.

Life's central vow of loving and being loved came home to my wife, Carolyn, and me with resounding clarity and power during a recent trip to the University of Notre Dame at South Bend, Indiana. Back in 1961, her father, Millard Sheets, was commissioned by the University President, Father Theodore Hesburgh, to design a mural to form the face of what was at that time to be the largest university library in the country.

Though we had seen postcards of this 160' by 40' granite mural, still the most massive of its kind anywhere in the entire world, we had never viewed it in person. So this was not just another trip but a true pilgrimage to honor Carolyn's father's stunning creation.

The University had graciously sent us printed and pictorial materials about the mural, so that we might ready ourselves for this 35-year-awaited visit. Preparation was important, but the actual moment of encounter boggled our spirits and surpassed our expectations.

One of Carolyn's brothers had spoken enthusiastically about the Notre Dame library facade being "the eighth wonder of the world," and although his sentiment could be dismissed as mere family hyperbole, the actual sight of Jesus—one of life's consummate teachers with his arms outstretched in forty-two foot wingspan—was simply staggering, overwhelming, drove us to silence and tears.

After Millard had designed this engineering and artistic masterpiece, it took a quarry in Minnesota over a year to cut the thousands of pieces of different colored granite. The mural is playfully known to rabid Notre Dame football fans across television land as "The Touchdown Jesus," because, with its upward reaching arms, the Nazarene is fantasized to be signaling a touchdown every time Notre Dame scores.

However, its proper name is the "Word of Life," and, in truth, it majestically depicts Jesus as religion's supreme teacher surrounded by scholars, saints, scribes from the Eastern and Western branches of Christendom. All the figures deferentially turn toward Jesus as the culminating presence.

In the New Testament, Jesus reportedly said "I am the way, the truth, and the life." Whether one considers Jesus to be the exclusive or an exemplary route to the good life, few of us would dispute that his central teaching was one of love. Jesus' major lesson was unequivocally loving and being loved.

Here at a midwestern academic institution, Roman Catholic to be sure, Jesus, the teacher of teachers, has been depicted with compassionate arms—welcoming travelers from all corners of the universe to come unto him for challenge and comfort. This imposing work of art claims that the apex of learning is love, that the fount of wisdom is love, that the summation of all the books contained in the very library to which Jesus is beckoning us...is love.

XIV

EROTIC NOT SEXY

People admit it's hard to pray. Yet they think it's easy to make love. What nonsense. Neither is worth much when it is only the outcropping of intermittent enthusiasm. Obviously the sexual act itself is central. But the circle that is drawn around it consists of a thousand small passes and light touches...a vast amount of incidental tenderness.

Robert Capon

Having sex is what the animals do. Achieving mystical union is what the angels do. We alone can make love, where the physical and the spiritual commingle in a single, joyous act.

Kent Nerburn

Love me little by little, be not in haste. For I would have you love me long. Love me slowly, love me deeply, love me long.

Salvador de Madraiaga

Love doesn't just sit there, like a stone, it has to be made, like bread; remade all the time, made new.

Ursula Leguin

Over thirty years ago during my training as a campus ministry intern at Beloit College in Wisconsin, I delivered a sermon that was warmly received by various folks. The Dean of the Chapel was so impressed that he advised me to send it off to *Pulpit* magazine for publication. However, first I should run it by his friend, Ed Warner, a former editor of *Pulpit*.

Warner scrutinized it, then called me over to his home for

comments. His words were blunt, almost blistering, to the ears of this green-horn seminarian: "Tom, your sermon is sexy but rarely erotic!" He proceeded to demonstrate convincingly where it was sexy: where the language was showy, even titillated the mind; where the style was shiny enough to sell and be bought; where the content swiveled and was succulent but failed to exude vitality; where the message aroused one without making connection; where the sermon crackled but couldn't sustain its blaze. His critique proved scathingly accurate not just about this lone sermon but my overall life at the time. Moreover, Warner evinced a truth about our greater society.

The lover, when fueled by eros, desires to touch and be touched with a primal knowing, beneath the surface, with inner passion. The trouble with most contemporary women and men is not that we feel too much passion, but that we don't access our passion sufficiently. We are disconnected from our erotic wellsprings. Sexiness by itself prompts us to be scintillating and juicy without risking concomitant warmth and ardor.

In Greek mythology, **Eros** appears as one of the four original gods, along with **Chaos, Gaea** (Mother Earth) and **Tartarus** (the dark pit of Hades below the earth). The legend goes that "Eros seized his life-giving arrows and pierced the cold bosom of Earth," and "Immediately the brown surface was covered with luxuriant green."

Eros supplies life-enhancing energy that infuses the creative, re-creative, pro-creative sharings of existence. Eros personifies the irrepressible yearning of humans to see higher and feel deeper as they refine their love-connections.

Eros started as a divine being. Later in Greek culture the concept of Eros deteriorated from the stature of the primal creative power to that of an insipid, frivolous, irresponsible, chubby child who played with bows and arrows. Psychoanalyst Rollo May called him a "banal playboy," bereft of significant tenderness or strength. In contemporary society we employ the word "erotic" almost entirely to describe lurid books and dirty films.

We moderns confuse eros with lust, yet they couldn't be more dissimilar. Lusting is selfish, uninvolved, insatiable, never reaching any goal. It craves and chases *ad nauseam*. As a mindset and mode of behavior, lust is considered one of the deadly sins, because it uses persons as objects for self-gratification. Eros, on the other hand, focuses upon affection and communion. It seeks durability and depth in its alliances.

As Henry Fairlie distinguishes:

> *Lust dies at the next dawn, and when it returns in the evening, to search where it may, it is with its own past erased. Eros wants to enjoy in other ways the human being whom it has enjoyed in bed! It looks forward to having breakfast together.*

As we enter the 21st century, we need to reappropriate the grandeur and power, the godliness, if you will, of Eros.

In scrutinizing the Greek words for expressions of love one discovers four: *agape* which represents charitable giving and unconditional compassion; *philia* which denotes friendship or companionship; *phylon* which refers to reproductive sexuality; and *eros* which constitutes the generative energy of creation and communion. Eros furnishes the energy for all loving. Without eros, agape degenerates into martyrdom. Without eros, philia becomes obligation. Without eros, phylon reduces to breeding.

In all of our loving endeavors, be they compassionate, sexual or friendly, the undergirding power must be erotic not sexy. The noun *sexus* was an invention of the Romans, probably derived from the Latin verb *secare*, which means "to cut or sever." Men and women have found in casual sexual liaisons that we are often cut off—heart from body, words from acts, sex from love, today from tomorrow. Cut off, cut up, cut out, we are frequently damaged without much to show for our sex except gnawing pain. Henry Miller, in describing sexual intercourse, put it poignantly:

> *If you enter deep enough, remain long enough, you will find what you seek. But you've got to enter with heart and soul and check your belongings outside.*

Sexual communion furnishes yet another hard blessing, because it requires time, commitment, passionate, surrender—eros permeating the core of our intimacy. In the Song of Solomon we read that quintessential passage of partnered love: "You are my beloved and you are my friend!" (5: 16) For partners who are equally friends and beloveds, the sexual experience can be a varied yet continual renewal of their sense of unity, one of life's enduring joys.

What does it mean to "make love"? To be sure, lovers may make noise, gyrations, babies, but love seems subtler, more mysterious, greater than the result of any behavior. During mutual sexuality, more love is *made* than existed before the given partners dared the intimacies of erotic communion.

Love is not made from scratch or in a vacuum, but rather created from gracious gifts, grown afresh within a familiar context, activated by common respect, and bathed in fun and laughter. Indeed, the Inuit people's term for making love means "to make laugh together." Yes, without acknowledging the gawkiness of love-making, sexuality quickly becomes a grim enterprise.

So, we don't fall in love or even find it. We make love, and in so doing, erotic intimacy brings us as close to God as we probably ever get. There is a rabbinical phrase that says that every time we walk down the street we're preceded by hosts of angels singing, "Make way, make way, make way for the image of God." What does it mean to be created in the image of God? Well, among many things, it means being creative in all we do, utterly creative all the way to the grave. Creative lovers, at heart and in body.

To celebrate their 50th wedding anniversary, a couple returned to their honeymoon hotel. After retiring, the husband said, "Darling, do you remember how you stroked my hair?" And so she stroked his hair. She reminded him of the way they cuddled, and so they did. With a sigh, she said, "Won't you nibble my ear again?" With that, the husband got out of bed and left the room. "Where are you going?" cried the upset wife. "To get my teeth!"

May we nibble on our lover's ears all the way home.

XV

YE SHALL RESPECT ONE ANOTHER

But, once the realization is accepted that even between the closest human beings infinite distances
continue to exist, a wonderful living side by side
can grow up, if they succeed in loving the distance
between them which makes it possible for each to
see the other whole and against a wide sky.

Rainer Maria Rilke

To say I love you is to say that you are not mine,
but rather your own. To love you is to advocate
your rights, your space, your self, and to struggle
with you, rather than against you, in our learning
to claim our power in the world. To love you is to
be pushed by a power/God both terrifying and comforting, to touch and be touched by you. To love
you is to sing with you, cry with you, pray with
you, and act with you to re-create the world. To
say I love you means—let the revolution begin!

Carter Heyward

I like to think that Jesus said in Aramaic, 'Ye shall
respect one another.' That would be sign to me that
He really wanted to help us here on Earth, and not
just in the Afterlife.

Kurt Vonnegut

I dream that love without tyranny is possible.

Andrea Dworkin

One of love's hardest blessings arrives whenever we honor the distance between us and our cherished ones, as Rilke encourages. Rather than ignoring or shrinking the distance, we must learn to juggle intimacy and apartness. Too much of the former and symbiosis strikes; too much of the latter and remoteness ensues.

I appreciate the way Chloe and Roger Housden honor creative distance in their marital bond:

> We are alone now even when we are together, though not in a way that makes us separate from each other. We look at one another sometimes and marvel at how utterly **other** we are to each other. The paradox is that now we are at home in our aloneness, we are joined in a way that is more complete than before. Rather than being submerged by our union, our individuality is enhanced by it.

Essential to loving the distance between individuals or groups is negotiating compromises on a regular basis. Every relationship requires yielding and shifting, time and time again, giving up something so that the overall union might be served. **Com-promise** means each partner promises to contribute something for the benefit of the larger relationship instead of abetting our separate egos. As my friend puts it: Being right is the booby prize, staying healthfully together is the objective of love.

Compromise is the trademark of the human species and a source of adaptability in our evolution. Only 15% of our brain is grown before birth, and 85% is developed afterwards, so we are far more adaptable than imagined. As one analyst noted about the grand achievements of Eleanor Roosevelt: "She mastered the art of compromising *up*!" Life and love are basically about compromise.

I read recently about the newly-formed Common Ground Network in Washington, D.C., that offers reconciliation efforts across the land between pro-life and pro-choice forces.

Common Ground is an approach to dialogue in highly conflictual situations. It emphasizes areas of agreement while respecting profound differences. Common Ground is not some mushy, middle ground, but a program that offers opponents a chance to move to "higher ground" by furnishing space "to sit down together, hear each others' stories and rehumanize people on the other side of the chasm."

In small groups, participants are invited to share the story of how they came to call themselves pro-choice or pro-life. You see, no one can argue with a person's experience. Frequently, the common denominator is a painful experience, and that's usually why there is so much passion around this issue.

Common Ground works for people who don't have to create an enemy in order to do their moral work. Common Ground majors in respect.

Bill Jones, a leading African-American theologian, in reflecting upon building respectful distance among the different races, put it succinctly: "The mission of racial justice is nothing less than the **co-equality** of individuals." I like his term co-equality. Neither assimilation nor integration are adequate to the task of fostering upright bonds; only co-equality is sufficient, since it regards the full worth and value of all persons involved. Co-equality is what the Buddhists mean when they recommend "right relations." Fairness must prevail in every minor detail and major task.

Respect is one of the most underpracticed aspects of a loving relationship. Gentleness is crucial, so is patience. Love withers without a sense of humor. But no quality is more critical to sustaining love than respect. Genuine respect in our families, friendships, workplaces, and partnerships is incredibly hard to come by, for it requires that we be more flexible and egalitarian than most individuals are on a daily basis. As Sam Keen puts it: "Respect is love at second sight." And third and fourth...

Real love is absent in any bond that isn't grounded in mutual respect. The crucial query stands: Can we look at one another and honestly say, "You and I are equally worthwhile creations. I hold you in the highest regard. Your time, your tasks, your needs, your visions are as significant as mine and will be treated as such in our relationship."

XVI
DURING THE DRAB INTERVALS

> Remember that all our failures are ultimately failures in love, but imperfect love should never be condemned or rejected.
>
> *Iris Murdoch*

> If we are to be pilgrims for justice, love, and peace, we shall not walk on roses, we must expect the desert.
>
> *Dom Helder Camara*

> My marriage, inspite of its ill-conceived beginnings and sometimes tumultuous course, has endured for 27 years. My husband smells right to me.
>
> *Diane Ackerman*

Love is mainly about picking oneself and one's relationship up after unavoidable lapses and crashes. Love loves even when the road is steep or jolting. Love keeps going when our buddies desert or revenge seems appealing.

Love weathers our foolish and foul intentions as well. We are incurably complicated creatures, and sound therapy and righteous attitudes can't cure the fact that, even in the most loving of bonds, our motives are checkered and our behavior faulty. As poet Mary Oliver candidly observes: "Mostly, I want to be kind, and nobody, of course, is kind or mean for a simple reason."

In John Irving's novel *The Hotel New Hampshire*, there is a beloved family hound called "Trouble." After Trouble dies, he is "stuffed," and retained as a family heirloom, accompanying them wherever they go. Even during a shipwreck, when all family baggage disappears overboard, Trouble floats on the surface. Trouble won't forsake the family. In a similar vein, pain or hardship never quite leave our loving bonds. Trouble merely resurfaces in unpredictable shapes and places.

Love is essential during life's times of extreme joy and adversity, but, perhaps, most necessary during the drab intervals. As Daniel Berrigan reminds us: "On a long drive, there's bound to be a dull stretch or two. Don't go anywhere with someone who expects you to be interesting indefinitely." All our loving, no matter how watchful, must withstand boring periods, when our zeal fades.

We can't help but be heartened by the honest testimony of Carl Rogers, one of the 20th century's most self-actualized psychologists, who confessed that his marriage survived a grisly bout with sexual sluggishness. Ellen Goodman likewise emboldens all intimates when she predicts: "Familiar fondnesses will win over familiar annoyances in a good partnership."

Everyone of us, both individually and relationally, will prove ineffectual at loving from time to time. We die before we reach the bulk of our goals anyway. However, our mission is not to succeed but to be constant, to remain as faithful as possible to what we hold dear. Remember, "loving means holding to the difficult."

Great composers don't set to work because they are inspired, but usually become inspired because they are working. Beethoven and Mozart settled down day after day to the task at hand with as much steadiness as an accountant settles down each day to her figures. They didn't waste time waiting around for motivation. They plodded. They persevered. They perspired. A great artist once said, after he had been working for eighteen years on a landscape, "The sky is getting interesting now!"

If we want a better society, we work at it, we plod. If we want more loving relationships, we work at them, we plod. If we want a more disciplined religious life, we work at it, we plod. While plodders make improvements, sprinters make dust.

Charlie Brown is walking along with his sister, and Sally, looking at her report card, remarks: "What kind of report card do you call this? I didn't even get any grades...All it says is 'Good Hustle.'" Well, when all is said and done, love's report card will include comments about "good hustle."

Lovers are lifers: we commit not for the short period but for the long haul, for life. We commit not perfectly, mind you, but steadfastly. Love isn't a one-time event. It isn't a means toward a distant end. Love is both the means **and** the end. Lovers recall that change is slow. They pursue excellence not flawlessness. Gutzon Borglum, the sculptor who created the tremendous Mount Rushmore Memorial, was once asked if he considered his work perfect in detail. "Not today," he replied. "The nose of Washington is an inch too long. It's better that way, though. It will erode to be exactly right in 10,000 years."

So, love is for the plodders and the patient, not the flashy or impulsive of spirit. This becomes clear when we realize that the word **compassion** can be read as *com-patience*, because the words passion and patience both find their roots in the same Latin word *pati*.

True patience is the opposite of passive waiting where we let things happen and allow others to make the decisions. Patience means to enter slowly but surely into the thick of love's challenge and then bear (as well as bare) the entire host of feelings within and around us.

Lovers never really get the chance to coast. They keep on keeping on...

XVII
JUST BE MY FRIEND

Friendship is the noblest and most delightful of all
the gifts the gods have given to humankind.
Cicero

Friendship is society's highest and holiest calling.
Mary Wollstonecraft

In a world plagued by gender misunderstanding—even
sexual violence, homophobia, and racism—friendship isn't
merely a nicety or luxury. It is an cardinal ingredient in the
salvation of our civilization. Same-sex and other-sex friendships are equally critical, but our most underdeveloped zone
has been intergender respectfulness. As one sociologist
phrased it, "Because of sexism, men and women can't be
friends. Because of sexism, men and women must be friends."

The dominant-submissive model of male-female relations
that has reigned supreme for centuries must be systematically
dismantled and replaced by what Riane Eisler calls "the way
of partnership," especially if we are interested in bequeath-
ing a millennium of gender justice to the boys and girls coming after us.

Sociologists tell us that "friendship is the third most important relationship in our lives, the one that's supposed to
be the icing on the cake." Partnership and family come first
and second. In truth, friendship is considerably more than an
hors d'oeuvre, more than parsley around the edges, more than
icing on the cake. A banquet that disregards friends as one of
its main dishes is a paltry, undernourishing meal indeed.

Some notes on the befriending process.

Friends come in all shapes, sizes, colors, and demeanors, including some pretty odd combinations. To muddle matters, engendering friendship banks considerably on good fortune, being the right person at the right place at the right time.

The duration of friendships is peculiar too. Some people are friends forever. Their attachment grows harmoniously, lasts. Other ties constitute fleeting, nonetheless powerful, encounters.

Moreover, we are rarely befriended by one person in all of our being. George Santayana was accurate in musing: "Friendship is almost always the union of a part of one mind with a part of another; people are friends in spots." And so, if we have several friends, most of our personality will eventually meander into the open. But we need to quit holding out for one buddy who will be everything for us. He or she probably doesn't exist. We would do well to settle for "friends in spots."

Additionally, there's an emotional geography to friendship. Camus put his finger on it: "Don't walk in front of me, I may not follow. Don't walk behind me, I may not lead. Walk beside me and just be my friend." Sometimes, friends lug us somewhere. They pick us up and take us places. Once in a while, they have been known to shove us from behind, to get our rears in gear. But, usually, the most pleasurable position for both parties is when we stride alongside our friend. There is mutuality. We are equal. Like partners in a dance, when things are going along swimmingly, we don't know who's leading and who's following. We don't even care.

Friendship isn't magical. It doesn't occur because we hunger for it. Friendships happen because two peers pay the price of authentic give-and-take. Friendship means spending quality moments, both being and doing together. Friends share projects, wage affectionate battles, celebrate life-passages. St. Exupéry put it elegantly:

Old friends cannot be created out of hand. Nothing can match the treasure of common memories of trails endured together, of quarrels and reconciliations and generous emotions. It is idle, having planted an acorn in the morning, to expect that afternoon to sit in the shade of an oak.

Friendships also call for openness. "A friend," said Emerson, "is a person with whom I may be sincere. Before a friend I may think aloud." Friends find it essential to understand one another, yet are able to frankly disagree. Good friends will scuffle with us, while shallow ones head for cover during conflict. Real comrades not only dislike what we do at times but periodically find us downright obnoxious and unlovely. They tell us so, yet continue to accept us. Substantial friendships must be continually patched and updated.

We all have fair-weather pals who wouldn't dream of going tiger-hunting with us in the jungle. And there are those so-called friends who have a need to parent or soothe us, invariably showing up when we're needy, down and out. They can't wait to try out their most recent psychological stratagem on us.

Such types are half-friends. They're sometimes just what we seek, but, most of the time, we hanker after full-fledged friends. We desire a handful of individuals who are emotionally ambidextrous, who can comfort or confront us with equal agility. Or simply disappear, if need be.

Finally, let's put friendship in historical perspective. For centuries male friendships set the measure for all human kinship. From Greek philosophers to modern writers such as Lionel Tiger, male bonding was deemed the model. Women's friendships were minimized as "too childlike, given to instability, to petty jealousies and trivial concerns."

Today, the tables have turned: women are considered the standard bearers for friendship, because they are socialized to be more emotionally revealing than men. Men are trained to be competitive and constrained, less agile in the arts of intimacy.

As we enter the 21st century, men and women are equally challenged to transcend such stereotypes. Neither gender is constitutionally inferior. Both women and men are innately capable of sharing hearts and displaying fondness.

Our culture majors in courtship and minors in friendship. In order for our relational nexus to prove more equitable and enjoyable, we need to reverse that pattern. "Love being difficult" bids us to share in the joys and challenges of both same-sex and other-sex friendships. Moreover, whether gay or straight or bisexual or transgendered, we are summoned to diversify beyond our primary partnerships.

We have a chance for the first time since pre-patriarchal history to migrate toward greater egalitarianism, to become soulmates as women and men, to say with undefended minds and friendly hands, "From you I receive, to you I give—tenderly and honestly—together we grow."

XVIII
MOST INTENSIVE COURSE

Being a good parent isn't just difficult, it's impossible. There is simply no way to be a good parent in
a society organized against children. The best things
that happen between parent and child happen by
accident or by surprise, very often breaking all rules.
Anyone who isn't bewildered by child-rearing and
doesn't find it an extremely formidable and trying
experience probably isn't a parent.

Richard Farson

Given America's nuclear family crisis, parenting is indeed
love's most intensive, if not severe, course. There are several tough lessons rarely mentioned in manuals, yet familiar
to practicing parents.

A first lesson. Although there is a resurgence of interest in
being a parent today, let's come clean—parenting is not for
everybody! Some adults don't feel sufficiently comfortable
around children to have their own. These are not bad adults
at all, and they should never be cajoled or shamed into becoming parents. Parenting is merely one way for adults to
shape culture and needs to be an unpressured choice.

Secondly, parenting cannot be accomplished effectively
alone or even as a couple, but requires the active support of
one's extended family, neighbors, friends, and religious community.

A third hard-won blessing that comes as a blow to some
parental egos is the realization that there are other adults circulating in our lives who can relate to our own children ex-
ceptionally well—even be and do things we parents can't be
and do. Consequently, it is prudent for parents to make the

following sort of pledge upon their child's birth:

> *We celebrate and welcome this new life that has come into ours. One of the lessons, you, our beloved child, will need to learn is about sharing and, we, your parents, need to learn this lesson, too. There are those around us who are entitled, nay invited, to be involved as you grow and change, and we need to feel secure enough to share you with them. Our parenting role in your world is distinct and irreplaceable, and remembering that can make our sharing you with others easier.*

Here's an apt metaphor for sound parenting. A good home provides the protection of sturdy walls and a sheltering roof, but windows and doors are also essential. Through windows our children glimpse a grander world and through doors come friends and strangers into their lives, full of instruction—sometimes good, sometimes bad.

A fourth tough yet necessary learning follows from the third one. We parents are *related* to our kids—be they natural, adopted, or step—but we are not ultimately *responsible* for them. Parents mistakenly want to take credit or blame for how our children turn out without allowing them to shoulder the bulk of their own credit or blame.

The desire to re-create the adult self through one's child can prove to be a devastating parental blind spot. Our children possess inalienable rights to become what they are capable of becoming, no matter how different from our blueprints.

As vehemently as I disagree with the message and methods of the Heaven's Gate cult, I was impressed with one of the mother's attitudes toward her wayward, certainly absent, son. David was an angry, volatile 19-year-old when he stumbled on a cult meeting in the park near his Los Gatos, California, home. The young man disappeared soon afterward, and for

21 years his mother tried to track him down, eventually organizing parent support groups. Finally, after seeing him twice during the intervening years, she accepted David's decision and even became proud that he had achieved the status of a certified computer network engineer.

Instead of rejecting David, she accepted her son and his choice as lovingly as she could. When interviewed after his death in the mass suicide of cult members, she commented: "It's been, I'd say, 21 years of losing, and the acute anguish doesn't end, yet David led a fairly dedicated, happy, fruitful life in the cult. How many parents can say the same?"

A fifth challenging parental reminder has to do with loving our children equally. When we don't, we either fail to admit it to ourselves or lug ourselves to the proverbial woodshed. One way out of this quandary is to confess: "I love my children differently rather than equally." We customarily love all our children, from beginning to end, but as Bruno Bettelheim indicates: "Love is not enough." Gratifying parenthood also requires liking or enjoying our children, and when honestly acknowledged, that attitude can vary markedly from child to child.

Whereas we take for granted that adults mesh with some adults and not with others, we expect equal levels of enjoyability with respect to our parent-child bonds. But the fact is that certain children are, on the whole, more agreeable than others to any given parent due to personality resemblance or relational rhythm or whatever. Some parents and children go together well, others don't.

Certainly, comparisons are odious, and I don't recommend telling particular children that we enjoy them more or less than the others, although, it's seldom a secret to any family member. Nonetheless, it's liberating for parents to know that we aren't lousy parent-people because we love our children differently and appreciate them unequally. And, of course, the same goes for children's sentiments toward their respective parents.

As long as we are swimming murky waters, let me drag us one fathom deeper. Most parenting primers announce that in parent-child squabbles, everyone can win, and furthermore, that any lingering bitterness or disappointment will eventually give way to love. That's our hope, but let's not be romantic. Often, the only way through familial pain is by directly confronting it, sometimes immersing ourselves in it.

In the Coptic (Egyptian) version of the New Testament is found a disturbing passage where Jesus declares that "No one can enter the realm of heaven until they have dealt with both their love and hate toward their parents." That's pretty blunt counsel coming from one of the peace-making sages of human history. But it furnishes keen emotional wisdom, for too many sons and daughters remain trapped all their days unable to release honestly held, ambivalent feelings toward either or both parents.

No parent-child relationship can ever be written off, for memories of love and possibilities of hope live on—and they should. I personally aspire, in all my interpersonal bonds, to heed the Hindu wisdom, namely: "Don't throw anyone out of your heart!" The right conditions, counseling, timing, and lots of good fortune have certainly sustained our own family through some dismal days and propelled us toward healing.

But we humans are destined to live with profound sorrows and irreconcilable severings everywhere in our existence, including our families. To scapegoat or second-guess either ourselves or our children merely aggravates the grief. The harsh reality remains that not all parent-child relationships have happy beginnings, middles, or endings. The key is to live with ambivalence and, if possible, to diminish any abiding resentment, instead of acting out or denying our shadow emotions.

The prevalent opinion is that the parent's job is to raise their children to be happy and responsible humans. I agree only in part. We parents don't *raise* children: We raise flags, blinds, arms, corn, but not humans. We foster a healthy environment and train ourselves as parents, but children, sooner or later, shape themselves. They may or may not decide to be happy and responsible persons, but whatever happens to them, our children must be measured by their own standards.

In the last analysis, the best parenting gift is our moral example. A teacher in Seattle, while the Cold War was still intense, asked his class of first graders how many thought there would be a nuclear war. All of the children except one raised their hands. The teacher was startled, but he was even more astonished that one child held out against all the others. So he asked, "Why don't you agree?" And the child answered: "Because my mother goes to a meeting every Tuesday night so that there won't be any war!"

It is an unmistakable delight when our children respond to our gifts of love. It is a thrill when they initiate their own. But their responses can't be predicted or programmed. There are no guarantees in love as in parenting, only opportunities to be seized.

The real joy and power in parenting understandably comes from mutuality. A girl and her father were walking along a road when they came across a large stone. The girl said to her father, "Do you think if I use all my strength, I can move this rock?" Her father answered, "If you use all your strength, I'm sure you can do it."

The girl began to push the rock. Exerting herself as much as she could, she pushed and pushed. The rock didn't move. Discouraged, she said to her father, "You were wrong, I can't do it." Her father placed his arm around the girl's shoulder and said, "No, Susie, you didn't use all your strength, you didn't ask me to help!"

Well, that's the fundamental blessing, isn't it? We parents and children need one another to accomplish all we might and must along life's rocky pathway.

XIX

WE MUST PERFORCE GO ALONE

Love consists in this, that two solitudes protect and
border and salute each other.

Rainer Maria Rilke

The deepest experience the soul can know—the birth
of a baby, the prolonged illness or death of a loved
relative, the torturous pain or the isolation of disease, the creation of poem, a painting, a symphony,
the grief of a fire, a flood, an accident—each in its
own way touches upon the roots of loneliness. In all
these experiences we must perforce go alone.

Clark Moustakas

We enter this world alone. We emerge from the womb,
naked, and yelping as we burst from sheltered solitude
into an exposed, noisy scene. We also exit alone, and even the
interlude between our birth and death—whether painful, boring, or happy—finds us alone. "Alone, alone, all alone, alone
on a wide, wide sea" wrote the poet Coleridge.

Naturally, we can share our experiences, and we do. We
impart feelings, exchange ideas, and intertwine bodies. We
unite spirits when task or tragedy calls. We can, moreover,
love someone from marrow to marrow. Nonetheless, when all
is said and done, we dwell alone within our ensouled body.
There are places in each of us that can never be visited even
by the closest of companions.

Contrary to popular opinion, love doesn't erase human loneliness. The romantic illusion persists that, at long last, in the
arms of another, our every desire will be filled. We frantically
cry out: "You, my love, are the only person for me. You are

70

my rock. Without you, my life would prove meaningless."

Such is not the cry of love but the shriek of desperation. Friendships and partnerships are frequently composed of two people who can't support their own well-being. Hence when we multiply one-half by another half, we end up with one-quarter, not a whole. That's a truism in math as well as in relationships. Another person can never make us complete. That's our own job. The purpose of a love-bond is to merge two evolving wholes not blend two faltering halves!

Only when we learn to salute rather than shun our solitude, can we reach out to another ready for love. Love may ease our aloneness, but love will never dissolve it. If there be any way to drown our sorrows, if there be any way to eliminate our loneliness, the solutions offered will never resemble love. We are frightened to live alone...alongside one another. Therefore, we bury our solitariness in the bosom of another.

To be sure, our devoted partners can love us, but they can't truly **adore** us; such uncritical adulation remains the province of the cats and dogs, and perhaps grandchildren, that populate our adult lives.

We humans are scared to love the infinite unknowns between us. "Love being difficult." But sincere love forces us to live imaginatively and courageously amid our aloneness. In our profoundest moments of communion, we live **beside** rather than **inside** another.

As Carl Sandburg says in the title of one of his poems: "Love is a Deep and a Dark and a Lonely." Carson McCullers pens a beautiful passage in her novel, *The Ballad of the Sad Cafe*, in which she puts to rest the myth that love is an antidote to the experience of being alone. Love, in fact, is a kind of loneliness, she writes. Love entails accepting the mystery of one's partner and refusing to violate that mystery. To clutch or shrivel the mystery of another person is tyranny.

We oft-cowering humans hanker for a tame love where our friend or partner mirrors what we like about ourselves. But if we love someone because they always please us, that's just a roundabout way of hugging ourselves.

It is a sign of great strength, rather than weakness, to let other people remain distinctly separate and not interfere with the choices they wish to make. Love is the ability to say No to everything that seeks to dilute intimacy into symbiosis—either shielding us from our own solitude or violating the privacy of another.

I started this essay by saying that we enter the world alone and leave the world alone. That's accurate but not the whole story. We were also born through and into relation, and we leave lasting influences when we die. Therefore, the other side of the paradox holds as well: communion creates us, and we depart in communion.

My family, my marriage, my religious fellowship all continue to remind me to commit my life, no holds barred, to being alone...together. Our existential condition is solitariness; our essential call is solidarity. We enact our destiny between these two fierce realities. Our loving becomes a lie, even hazardous to our health, if either truth of this paradox is violated.

XX

CARING IS EVERYTHING

In the sense in which a person can ever be said to be at home in the world, we are at home not through dominating, or explaining, or appreciating, but through caring and being cared for...

Milton Mayeroff

The physician's (caregiver's) task is to cure rarely, relieve often and comfort always.

Oliver Wendell Holmes

We were loved into existence beyond our merit; our finest response, while alive, is to love in return by supporting fellow-travelers in need, by healing the environment, by befriending animals, by accompanying the Great Spirit. Yet, as John Corrado warns: "Caring is easy to talk about, but caring is not easy."

One of love's trickiest teachings is how to become effective caregivers—whether assisting someone suffering from a broken leg or a broken heart, from a forsaken hope or a forsaken child, lost innocence or lost will. We start by aligning ourselves with Holmes' insight that our primary job is not to cure but to comfort others. **Comfort** literally means "to stand firm alongside another."

Comforting invites no showy performance. It doesn't require miracle workers or nursing professionals. It harkens for caring people. The very word "care" has its roots in the old Gothic term "kara," which means to lament. The real meaning of care, then, has to do with shared grieving, empathetically experiencing the pain of another, then choosing to be present.

The lover's mission is to be a caregiver not a caretaker. As such, we are willing to reach out and touch, ready to serve not solve another's ache. We care, despite our own frailties, knowing well that all of us are "wounded healers."

Caregiving exemplifies balanced and fair, non-possessive and non-exploitative love, marked by firm not leaky boundaries. Love is abundant; there is plenty to go around, if we share it judiciously.

However, it is tempting, as diligent caregivers, to fall prey to the subtle malaise of "helpaholism," caricatured in one of Virginia Glascow's novels: "She loved to help others. You could tell the others by their hunted look!" It is seductive to set ourselves up in a superior position of being the helper with others being helpees. The helpaholic mentality surfaces whenever we assist others to cover up our own pain. Whenever we are driven, desperate, or foster dependencies, our helping is counterproductive for everyone.

Caregivers realize that we are partners in our neighbor's healing process but refuse to don the rescuer complex. Doing for others what they can do for themselves insures their not growing accountable for their own life. It is a messianic illusion that we are indispensable to another person. That reminds me of the "Momma" cartoon strip where the overbearing mother says to her son: "Well, as long as I only have one life to lead, it's going to be *yours*!"

A minister friend of mine has on her desk four printed reminders: (1) Show up; (2) Pay attention; (3) Tell the truth; and (4) Let go of the outcome. Number four is the downfall of the helpaholic. Genuine caregivers hold on to our loves lightly, then relinquish the results. Buddhism has to do with right **action** but never right **results**. We cannot forecast the outcome of a relationship or a caring deed.

Caregivers know the transformative power of unaffected touching. Holding a hand means a great deal to someone fighting fear and isolation. The caress of one compassionate person is a gift of healing. When appropriate, we can offer a hug, for as Virginia Satir says: "We all need four hugs a day for survival, eight for maintenance, twelve for growth."

Once during our all-church camp, I asked the gathered families if they knew of anyone who was suffering. After moments of nervous silence, a bold teenager raised her hand and blurted out, "My father is, but he won't tell anyone!" She then tightly hugged her father who happened to be sitting next to her.

The father, already embarrassed, said, "Ginny, stop hugging me. You're hugging me to death." "Oh, no, Dad," Ginny cried, "I'm hugging you to life!" That's precisely what many people covet more than anything else. They desperately need to know that somebody cares. They need someone to hug them to life.

Caregivers are also summoned to listen. There's a reason we were graced with two ears and only one tongue. As one person in need so fervently reminds us:

When I ask you to listen to me and you feel you have to do something to solve my problems, you have failed me, strange as that may seem. All I asked was that you listen not talk or do. Just hear me. I can do for myself. I am not helpless, maybe discouraged and faltering, but not helpless. So please listen and just hear me. And, if you want to talk, wait a minute for your turn, and I'll listen to you.

We human beings come alive through caring. When Baron von Hugel, the great philosopher and mystic was dying, his niece could see his lips moving but could not catch what he said. So she put her ear close to his mouth and heard the last words that von Hugel ever uttered: "Caring is everything, nothing matters but caring!"

XXI
GUILT MATTERS

> Without guilt what is a human being? Guilt matters, guilt always must matter. Unless guilt matters, the whole world is meaningless?
>
> *Archibald MacLeish*

Guilt is a human experience as old as Adam hiding from God in the Garden of Eden. And recall the words of Jesus spoken to the gathered crowd, prepared to stone the woman caught in adultery: "Whoever is without sin, let them cast the first stone." The subsequent walking away of every assembled person is a striking image of universal guilt.

Yet there is bad guilt and good guilt. If guilt makes us feel utterly inadequate, then it is inhumane. If it causes us to see ourselves as dirty rags, or "miserable offenders" (as one prayer book puts it), then such guilt will leave scars that may never heal. But not all remorse is harmful or destructive. In modern society many of the old guilts are thrown off and rightfully so. But, at the same time, compunctions are often brushed aside, and little remains sacred. Guilt over neglected beliefs is harmful; guilt over ignored duties is valid.

Those who know love will feel guilt. Guilt is the warning tension that comes when life principles are betrayed, when relationships are violated, when conditions of social existence are transgressed, when the natural world is harmed, when the self is sabotaged. In sum, we are susceptible to feeling properly guilty whenever we wrong ourselves, others, or the universe.

Good guilt is what German philosopher Martin Heidegger named "the call of our conscience." It triggers an awareness of the creative tension between personal autonomy and social responsibility. It is the necessary goad that urges us to budge from moral ruts. Good guilt helps us show scruples in composing mature relationships. Good guilt reminds us that we stand accountable for what we do with who we are!

There is the Zen story of the ardent seeker after Truth. The roshi announces: "If what you seek is Truth, there is one thing you must have above all else." "I know," offers the seeker. "An overwhelming passion for it!" "No, no, more than that you need an unremitting readiness to admit you may be wrong!" Lovers need conscience-pain, we need to confess culpability, we need an ever-present sense of right and wrong.

Humans benefit from feeling good guilt whenever we justify deception or allow truth to rest quiet. We benefit from feeling good guilt about the casual way we treat our primary bonds. We benefit from feeling good guilt whenever we disrupt the delicate balance of the ecosphere. We benefit from feeling good guilt whenever we're content to see the mediocre become the ideal.

We need to feel guilt not because we're bad or defective beings, but because we are co-partners with the Creator in sustaining a lovelier, more peaceful, and just universe. And we cannot shirk that call. We throw away guilt, and civilization succumbs to anarchy. If we cauterize our moral sensibility, we subvert human community. It is unwise to sever nerves to eliminate pain. We need those nerve fibers.

Lest there be any confusion, guilt remains both a horrible and hopeful fact of our humanity. Present too constantly or too oppressively, it can lead to illness. Yet experiencing healthy conscience pain, we human beings are capable of the highest reaches of compassion and kinship. Lovers aspire to live with the right amount of guilt!

A brilliant movie in the 1990's depicting the interwoven themes of greed, guilt, and goodness was *Schindler's List*, by Steven Spielberg. This powerful film on the Jewish holocaust generates multiple learnings for those who feel guilt so fiercely because we love life so dearly.

Oskar Schindler was a German Catholic businessman and confidant of the Nazis, who, during the Holocaust, protected and rescued some 1200 Jews from almost certain death. In Poland today, where Schindler once ran his profitable enamelware factory during World War II, there are fewer than 4,000 Jews left.

Around the world there are more than 6,000 descendants of the "Schindler Jews" he saved. But to this day, nobody can say with certainty what made this improbable hero risk his life when so many others failed to lift a finger. Was it guilt, greed, goodness, or was it a combination of these sentiments?

Schindler was a hedonist of the highest order: a heavy drinker, a womanizer, and an shameless gambler. Schindler was also a polished, congenial man who may have been motivated by nothing more complicated than simple decency, but as we know, morality was neither simple nor easy to find among prominent German citizens in Eastern Europe between 1939 and 1945.

As commentator David Ansen reflects:

> To any sane observer, there has always been an unfathomable mystery about the systematic evil the Nazi regime perpetrated: like a moral black hole, it seems to defy the laws of nature while being a part of that nature. But sometimes the good is equally mysterious. The conscience of Oskar Schindler is a wonderful conundrum.

In the historical novel by Thomas Keneally, on which the movie was based, Schindler was essentially a slave-camp profiteer. Keneally writes: "You add up all the elements—the expediency and the decency—and you don't get the sum of what happened. Ultimately, Schindler had no motive except the desire to create a haven." Following the war, when pressed, the real Schindler would only say, "There was no choice." The stunning truth is that both before and after the war Schindler lived a thoroughly uninspired life.

Oskar Schindler was neither saint nor scoundrel, and, therewith, more like the rest of humanity than not—a complex blend of greed and guilt and goodness. His ambivalent human nature is what makes the movie so uncannily relevant to everyone of us who is flawed yet committed to the moral struggle to create a better world. The fundamental message of *Schindler's List* comes directly from the Talmud: "Whoever saves one life, saves the world entire!"

Schindler's List not only addresses a monumental tragedy of some 50 years ago, nor merely signals travesties of "ethnic cleansing" still practiced in our modern world, but the movie also speaks unerringly to everyone who walks the earth. It hammers away at the depths of our consciences, reminding us of the countless ways in which we can destroy and can heal our most basic, human bonds whether at work or home, during play or strife.

In this movie as in our lives, "There is nothing human that is alien to us!" Nothing horrible and nothing holy is foreign to our genius. Each of us contains the entire breadth of greed, guilt, and goodness in our innermost temples.

Such is the blessing and curse of human beings who dare to love.

XXII

LET YOUR LAUGHTER RING FORTH!

> Keep fightin' for freedom and justice, beloveds, but don't you forget to have fun doin' it. Lord, let your laughter ring forth!
>
> *Molly Ivins*

Love requires a cheerful spirit, resounding with laughter and brimming with silliness. Lovers radiate a kinesthetic spirituality where their innards bounce and swivel. The challenges of love are too important to be left to those who know not the company of clowns. Love is serious without being austere, zany without being inane.

In the Old Testament legend, Elisha hankers to be Elijah's disciple. After working together awhile, Elijah announces he will be leaving Elisha since God is taking him up to heaven in a whirlwind. In parting, what would Elisha need from him as mentor and friend? Elisha was crystal-clear in his request: "I would like a double portion of your spirit!" Elisha sought to be a prophetic presence full of joy and verve, energized by a sense of playfulness. Lovers bank on what Elijah ensouled, a double portion of spirit!

There is the parable about the Master who was in an exuberant mood, so his disciples sought to learn the stages he had endured in his quest for the divine. "God first led me by the hand," he said, "into the Land of **Action**, and there I dwelt for several years. Then God returned and led me to the Land of **Sorrows**; there I lived until my heart was purged of excessive attachment. That is when I found myself in the Land of **Love**, whose burning flames consumed whatever was left in me of overweening ego. This brought me to the Land of **Si-**

80

lence, where the mysteries of life and death were unveiled before my eyes."

"Was that the final stage of your quest?" they asked.

"No," the Master said. "One day, God said, 'Today I shall take you to the innermost sanctuary of the Temple, to the heart of God itself.' And I was led to the Land of **Laughter**!"

Merriment personifies what it means to be both robustly human and harmonious with the sacred. Only when love honors both its serious and funny sides will it remain secure in human hands. Mature individuals find ways to poke fun at the flaws of our foibled loving. We can jest about matters precious and important.

Being cheerful is an end in itself not just a means to regenerate the body or replenish the soul, to win friends or deepen relationships, even to beat depression or please the gods. We are playful animals by nature. We are here on earth, among other things, to play for play's sake—not to play with a Why in mind, with an opponent, or with a finish line. We are by nature frolicking, fun-loving creatures. Walter Bagehot reminds us that recreation instead of education may be closer to the divine plan: "Humans made schools, but God made schoolyards!"

Pablo Casals in his elder years got up every morning to play the piano not to flaunt his talent, which was considerable, not merely to keep physically active and mentally sharp, although that was part of his ritual as well. Casals played—and we play every day alone or together—to live. Or is it live to play?

It doesn't really matter, for love and playfulness are linked, from cradle to grave.

XXIII

DANGER
TO EVERY REPRESSIVE ORDER

We must accept finite disappointment, but we must never lose infinite hope...for the moral arc of the universe bends toward justice.

Martin Luther King, Jr.

Love is the birthright of every person.

Mother Teresa

Fair people do keep their commitments, give fair gifts and forgive fairly. Try love as fairness. Life isn't fair, but love can be.

Edward Harris

It is enticing for the "sweethearts" among us to be exemplary lovers in the comfort zones of our lives (such as among family and friends), then turn chicken-hearted when love requires us to venture beyond our secure havens. But lovers can't be choosers. We are summoned to build justice and make peace where it is unpopular, maybe dangerous..."love being difficult." George Leonard was on target when he remarked: "Love is a clear and present danger to every repressive order."

The energy of revolutionary love enables women and men to become advocates and allies for growing justice in the larger world. Along with Marian Wright Edelman, prominent Director of the Children's Defense Fund, lovers are determined "to make justice my life-calling."

Whether we are members of an oppressed group or dwell among the oppressors, or comprise a convoluted mix of the two, our moral imperative is to emerge from closets of hostility and fear and to grow closer encounters of fondness and trust. Episcopalian theologian and lesbian activist Carter Heyward notes: "The closet is a container designed to impede the movement of an erotically empowering sacred Spirit and to silence her voices."

When Thucydides was asked if justice would ever come to Athens, the Greek historian replied, "Justice will not come to Athens until those who are not injured are as indignant as those who are injured." Centuries later the battle still rages for justice and dignity. This is no era to wallow in neutrality, spectating from the sidelines. Instead it is the epoch for fellow-travelers to break silence and engage in resistance. Allies aspire to be good neighbors in the fullest sense of the biblical phrase, inquiring of their sister or brother: "What do you need from me, and let's see if I can deliver it to you?"

To be an ally in justice-building requires steadfast courage. When Krushchev delivered his famous denunciation of the Stalin era, someone in the Congress Hall is reported to have said, "Where were you, Comrade Krushchev, when all these innocent people were being slaughtered?"

Krushchev stopped, looked around the Hall and said, "Will the person who said that kindly stand up?" Tension mounted in the Hall. No one stood up. Then Krushchev said, "Well, you have your answer now, whoever you are. I was in exactly the same position then as you are now!"

Being an ally means insisting that racism and class elitism, homophobia and sexism—and all other pernicious structures of bigotry, named and unnamed, in which we flounder—be eradicated. Being an ally means declaring by our deeds that injustices are indivisible and mutually reinforcing and need to be opposed in the open.

Being an ally means speaking out about the unearned privileges we enjoy as members of any dominant group—privileges we have been taught for so long to deny or ignore. As African-American colleague Alma Crawford prompts us: "Just

never forget that you Whites have been the nonstop benefi-
ciaries of the most effective Affirmative Action program in
history!"

Being an ally means not laughing at a derogatory joke. It
means challenging harassment when we see it. It means using whatever power we have to move justice forward, at work
or at play, with respect to legislation.

But we must surrender delusions of grandeur: There is no
such thing as a perfect ally. Allies are neither saints nor sav-
iors; our aim is to remain consistently conscious. Progress not
perfection is the intent of lovers as truth-tellers and justice-
builders. We will stumble, but if we admit when we lapse and
apologize when we show cowardice, we can always climb back
on the path.

Those persons who stood up against the Nazis, the "good
ones" if you will, gathered after the war to repent and confess
their complicity in evil, because they knew that they did not
do enough. In thus repenting, they were able to push through
guilt toward satisfactory healing.

Lani Guinier reminds us: "It is better to be vaguely right
than precisely wrong." If we focus on looking good instead of
doing good, we will be derailed. Lovers are summoned to be
our best selves, transforming the world one individual at a
time, one family at a time, one congregation at a time, one
community at a time, starting today with ourselves.

Beleaguered individuals must dare to be advocates for their
own dignity and destiny. And those in power, the privileged
gender, class, race or orientation—our mandate is to be allies.
Advocates alone can't create a just and merciful world, neither can allies, but together, as the spiritual goes, "we can
move mountains;" oh yes, we can move mountains.

As lovers we cannot wait for another place or another day
or another incarnation. One of our greatest modern poets,
Adrienne Rich, has written with severe truthfulness about
20th-century calamity and triumph, including piercing reflec-

tions upon both World War II and Vietnam. She sets a moral compass for our journey into the new millennium:

My heart is moved by all that I cannot save; so much has been destroyed. I have to cast my lot with those who, age after age, perversely, with no extraordinary power, reconstitute the world.

If her appeal sounds too mighty, then let us perversely reconstitute the small corner of the universe where we live. Or reconstitute our vision that we and all those whom we touch might have life, and life abundant.

XXIV
YOUNG AND OLD TOGETHER

Love comes quietly, softly, drops about me, on me
in the old ways. What did I know? Thinking myself
able to go alone all the way.

Robert Creeley

Hillary Clinton envisions a world in her book, *It Takes A Village*, where "there is no such thing as other people's children." Instead, we band together as spiritual relatives, promising one another our staunch regard and devotion. None of us—children, youth, or adults—belongs to one another anyway; we only hold one another on temporary loan. Her perspective recalls the tender story told by Ann Freeman Price, entitled: "A Miracle Under 34th Street."

A mother with her little boy of four or five got onto a New York City subway car. Soon after they had found seats almost facing each other, the train's rhythmic rolling soothed the little one to sleep. As the youngster nodded off, he leaned against the man sitting next to him. The man signaled to the mother that it was all right with him for the little boy to snuggle there beside him.

However, after a while, the man prepared to leave the train. By this time, the train was packed and people were standing in the aisles. The man motioned to another passenger. Without uttering a word the deal was struck. The seated man gently held the boy's head and slid out into the aisle while the second man slipped into place, cradling his head in its original position. The mother smiled. The boy shifted a little, then slept on.

That story superbly illustrates the blessing of

intergenerational community. The grown-ups among us stand ready to receive the little ones who dwell outside our homes, who roam beyond our designated care, who just might be transferred at any given moment onto our laps.

"Love being difficult" entails weaving an interdependent and intergenerational web that includes the distinct gifts of each age. We adults cannot treat children and youth as being of less value without faulting on our love. We are urged to relate to one another, across the generations, as persons of equal value and due full respect. No questions asked, no exceptions granted. For, as Holly Near's song goes, "We are young **and** old together, and we are singing, singing for our lives..." and one might add: rejoicing, struggling, yelling, loving for our very lives.

Have you seen the Bumper Sticker that reads: "The most radical thing we can do is introduce people to one another"? Lovers travel beyond introductions; we exhort sisters and brothers to spend actual time with one another across racial and class lines, as gays and straights, young and old. The window of time we young and old have together passes so quickly, the gulf remains so incalculable, the yearning is so profound. We owe one another not so much a piece of our minds (although that's part of the bargain), but a sizable portion of our time and our embrace. We owe one another, young and old, what H. L. Mencken called a "terrible loyalty"—terrible as in urgent, scary yet wonderful.

Children and youth covet adults who, most of all, have the courage to be authentic: adults who are vulnerable and open as well as strong and reliable; adults who are consistently caring even when they disagree or dwell in a crabby mood; adults who are willing to confront violations of mutual respect; adults who will remain stable presences in the lives of youth because they are quite comfortable with their own adulthood.

Our younger ones do not want glad-handers, marshmallows, or reflections of themselves. They sorely wish to be just

who they are—children and youth—and they can best be themselves whenever we adults are adults: distinct yet equal partners in creating a mutually resourceful intergenerational universe.

XXV

SHAKING HANDS WITH THE DRAGONS

> We have no reason to mistrust our world, for it is not against us. Has it terrors, they are our terrors; has it abysses, those abysses belong to us; are dangers at hand, we must try to love them... Perhaps all the dragons of our lives are princesses who are only waiting to see us once beautiful and brave. Perhaps everything terrible is in its deepest being something helpless that wants help from us.
>
> *Rainer Maria Rilke*

I consider the New Testament wrong when it claims that "perfect love casts out fear." First off, we humans never give or receive perfect love. Ours is always a sullied approximation. Perfect love doesn't exist on earth, and if it did, would it rid us of our fears, or, more likely, enable us to live more effectively amid them? It is critical along the loving path to hug our monsters and to shake hands with the dragons, as the Chinese urge.

My personal experience is that the deeper closeness I brave with another person, the scarier it gets. True intimacy is prickly, even abrasive. When downright honest, I both delight in and am terrified by the power that we loving people possess to harm one another. The words **sacred** and **scared** are identical, except for the transposition of one letter. It's a fruitful twist, because when lovers face what scares us, we are treading on sacred ground.

There is dread at the bottom of love. Comfort, security, communion, yes, but an ineradicable gloom as well. One by one our defenses are stripped to allow another person to enter the citadel of our privacy. And that's a scary bargain. The more my lover or friend views the real me, the more room for judgment, perhaps rejection. Intimates hold potential to aid in expanding or annihilating one another. If we don't care, nothing can hurt or frighten us. But if we do care, everything can. In matters of love, ecstasy and terror go hand in hand.

In the last analysis, we are loving beings because, in part, we are anxious beings. Love, bathed in creative apprehension, enables us to avoid dumb moves. Anxiety is frequently the goad propelling us beyond stagnation toward growth that will strengthen our bonds and improve society.

In the great American epic saga *Moby Dick*, the chief mate Starbuck says to his crew: "I will have no person in my boat who is not afraid of a whale." And Herman Melville goes on to say:

> *By this Starbuck seemed to mean not only was the most reliable and useful courage that which arises from the fair estimation of the encountered peril, but that an utterly fearless person is a far more dangerous comrade than a coward.*

Loving individuals experience activating not paralyzing fear. Loving relationships bank on nervous juices and are filled with sufficient angst. Fear never leaves us; may we learn to befriend it.

XXVI
SURRENDERING

When we were children, we used to think that when we were grown-up, we would no longer be vulnerable. But to grow up is to accept vulnerability. To be alive is to be vulnerable.

Madeleine L'Engle

Love is an attempt to penetrate another being, but it only can be realized if the surrender is mutual. It is always difficult to give oneself up; few persons anywhere ever succeed in doing so, and even fewer transcend the possessive stage to know love for what it actually is: a perpetual discovery, an immersion in the waters of reality, and an unending re-creation.

Octavio Paz

Among love's precarious blessings is developing bonds where the involved parties are vulnerable and open without being exposed and unstable. Theologian Howard Thurman states love's stubborn paradox with clarity:

What had I learned about love? Somewhere deep within was a place beyond all faults and virtues that had to be confirmed before I could run the risk of opening my life up to another. To find ultimate security in an ultimate vulnerability, this is to be loved.

In describing skillful guitar-playing my friend expresses it similarly: you must develop adequate calluses so that your fingers won't bleed, but not such hardened ones that you no longer feel the strings. Lovers possess the knack of growing the proper thickness of callus, just right for plucking melodious tunes.

Human pilgrims often seek a level of safety that permits minimal openness. We wrongly equate love with servitude, sacrificing our unique beings on the altar of unfreedom. Such pseudo-love becomes an excuse to abandon one's own identity or a justification for controlling that of another.

Remember that Rilke counsels that love entails *holding* to the difficult. Holding means grasping lightly rather than gripping tightly. False love resembles clinging rather than collaborating. Instead of squeezing the juices out of a relationship, love would hold, then release, its dancers in rhythmic measure.

Love travels the middle way of liberating commitments, bonds without bondage. Loving people give themselves over to one another as friends or intimates without giving themselves away. Surrender not subjugation.

It is no accident that the word *love* from the Latin word *amor* is close to the Greek word *amusso*, meaning "to choke." It is tempting to suffocate one's companion or to allow them to throttle our own free-flowing energy. All this "choking" perverts the name of love. On the contrary, beneficial loving keeps our freedom intact. As the Indian poet Rabindranath Tagore muses: "Let my love so surround you yet give you illumined freedom."

Part of love is an eagerness to vault beyond the familiar and comfortable into foreign territories of bold surrender. Poets know about this: "Love is plunging into darkness toward a place that may exist," (Marge Piercy) and "love's function is to fabricate unknown-ness." (e. e. cummings)

Surrendering is at the heart of the lover's bond with Divine Mystery as well. In my religious adolescence I clung to God in a way that didn't do justice to either of us. Then I rebelled against God and retreated into self-sufficiency. Now, although vowing never to **enslave** myself to any power, I am willing to **surrender** to the Creation. Everyday I surrender gladly, in love, to the various inexplicable mysteries of my vocation, my marriage, my parenting. I can explain them no more satisfactorily than I can explain deity.

Lovers willingly surrender our hearts and souls to a companionable presence with whom we can play, wrangle, and labor to co-create an evolving universe. Sometimes we call that reality God, sometimes we don't; sometimes we desire to talk or write about it, other times we keep quiet and simply gambol in the mystical embrace of partnership.

XXVII

BLESSED ARE THEY WHO MOURN

> I wonder why love is so often equated with joy when it is everything else as well. Devastation, balm, obsession, granting and receiving excessive value, and losing it again...the small pains as well as the great, it sears and it heals.
>
> *Florida Scott-Maxwell*

Authentic love knows tears as well as fears, both anguish and angst. Sufi poet and chanter Doug von Koss has vowed that whenever the flow of tears comes, he will let them wet his cheeks, then tumble, unwiped, to the ground.

There is good biblical support for crying. Near the end of that torturous tale of intrigue, betrayal, and forgiveness between Joseph and his brothers, Joseph is so overcome with emotion, particularly feelings of fondness for his kin, that he dissolves in tears. Joseph weeps, not once, twice or three times, but on six different occasions.

And in the New Testament, it is curtly reported: "And Jesus wept." This may be the shortest verse in the Bible, but what a mighty phrase! Jesus was distraught over the rotten behavior of his people, and instead of ranting and railing, instead of drafting an oration, instead of marshaling forces to mount a political response, he was simply moved to tears. He wept. Sometimes falling to pieces is the only way to put our selves back together again.

We weep tears of grief when a beloved dies, we weep tears of disappointment when a relationship ends, we weep tears of compassion upon leaving the hospital room of a seriously ill friend. Even those who seldom cry for personal reasons may be brought to tears in the dimness of a theater watching a stirring movie or play. Some people deliberately seek out four-handkerchief tearjerkers just so they can have a good cry.

We Americans, especially men, are notorious for trying to tough things out. Our problem is too little weeping for our own good. The cost is often great, as one physician aptly states: "Sorrows that find no vent in tears may soon make other organs weep."

We cry because we love. The wetter the better.

One of the pivotal mantras in my own sacred quest is contained in that familiar passage from the New Testament: "Blessed are those who mourn for they shall be comforted." So many lovers want to bypass pain and scamper unscathed toward the land of bliss. But without a healthy dosage of anguish in our lives, our relationships deliver erratic pleasure and insufficient solace. Why? Because comfort only comes to those courageous enough to mourn openly and ongoingly.

In counseling I find numerous individuals who have led emotionally constricted lives because they have been harboring a hurt or stifling an affection. As soon as they give voice to their buried feelings through sighs and tears—sounds deeper than words—they find release.

One evening Buddha heard wailing in a house he was passing and, upon entering quietly, he found that the householder had died and his family and neighbors were weeping. Immediately, Buddha sat down and began crying too. An elderly gentleman, shaken by this show of distress in such a famous guru, remarked: "I would have thought that you, the Buddha, at least, were beyond such emotional outbursts!" "But it is precisely this that puts me beyond it," Buddha replied through his sobs.

XXVIII
LISTENING TO THE SILENCES

The first duty of love is to listen.

Paul Tillich

All I know of love is that love is all there is.

Emily Dickinson

Observing the biblical injunction, to "speak the truth in love...", is vital to loving communication. Nonetheless, honesty is an instrumental value, not a terminal one. Being truthful must always stand in service of love. Consequently, there are portions of our beings that we neither can nor should divulge even in the most intimate of bonds. Sometimes, the better part of valor, wisdom, and love is to hold our tongues.

Unquestionably, one of love's paramount lessons is to discern when words are necessary and when they are futile, potentially harmful. A Jewish proverb implies that the deeper the love, the less tongue it hath.

Healthy communication requires both caring disclosure and sensible hush. Being an open book to one's lover is neither a possible nor a desirable goal. After all, even open books never reveal more than two pages at any given time.

An Hasidic tale recounts the initial meeting of two young rabbis. They retire to a room and seat themselves opposite one another. Face to face they sit alone in silence for a whole hour. In due time they announce to each other: "Now, we're ready to talk!" Whether in family encounters, business deals, friendships, or international confabs, loving individuals should choose to spend as much time preparing in silence as we do in conversation.

Most partnerships of over 50 years duration will confess that much of their valued interaction arrives by body language—a nod, a gesture, a look, especially a look—without benefit of words. In Buddhist tradition there are some 21 different terms for "silence." Resourceful couples are familiar with an infinite variety of forms of quietude.

Onlookers shouldn't feel sorry for couples who have been together so long that they don't say much when they go to restaurants. Of course, it could be a matter of deteriorating hearing or sometimes a matter of screening one another out. But often silence is the surest gift of love. Friends and lovers are nourished by routine word-fasts.

When our marriage was unsettled some years back we sought counseling. One of the most useful lessons we already knew but needed to learn again was the power of listening beneath chatter. Our therapist kept driving home the point that Carolyn and I should listen intently to every word the other was saying, but, more importantly, listen to every word not being spoken. She urged us to heed the nuances of our partner's being, to listen lovingly to the silences.

The Shona culture of Zimbabwe in Southern Africa espouses the concept of *rufaro* that roughly translates as contentment. Rufaro insinuates more than happiness, even satisfaction; it denotes a bedrock feeling of equilibrium. *Rufaro* is the desired destiny of every relationship. Those persons who experience *rufaro* harbor a profound sense of serenity no matter how life has treated them. They find fulfillment not only in their familial bonds but also with the larger community. Frustrated by life's daily inequities and tussles, a rufarian consciousness grounds lovers. While not resting on our laurels, we repose secure in the universe, content being still and silent.

Entering the silence is a holy vow available to all of God's lovers. The Greek root MYS in the words "mystery" and "mystic" means shutting the eyes, ears, or mouth, because in the presence of wondrous and awful things, we are driven to silence. Hence the sacred enterprise summons us to be mute and dumb sometimes, to still our mouth, then our mind, finally our will, to shut up fully before we dare to open up freshly to the bidding of the Spirit. It calls us to enter the silence, so the mystery within us might connect with the mystery beyond us.

XXIX
THREE REQUIREMENTS

What does the Lord require of you, but to do justice,
and to love kindness and to walk humbly with your
God?

Micah 6: 8

The book of the prophet Micah marks a watershed in the evolution of religion when we moved from animal sacrifices to human service, from ritual worship to social righteousness. If one pays heed to Micah's three imperatives of justice, kindness, and humility, then one's house of love will definitely be in order.

Micah contends that these ethical demands appear from beyond our ego or imagination. They come from the Eternal, from God, from the Creation. They are not intriguing, optional challenges we have dreamed up. They are what is expected, make that *required*, during our earthly adventure. They are transcendent claims on human life.

The first imperative is **"to do justice."** Not to think or visualize justice but to *do* some justice every waking day of our lives, not merely when we feel like it. Justice entails mending a broken world by making sure that what belongs to people gets to them: be it freedom, dignity, or resources.

As Matthew Fox reflects:

Injustice is a rupture in the universe, an affront to cosmic wholeness, an invitation to chaos, an unraveling of the ropes that bind the universe as whole. It is by justice that we bring together the broken, neglected, cut-off, impoverished parts of the universe to render them whole again.

My mother recently recounted a personal incident of justice-building that stirred me deeply. This is not the kind of anecdote my demure mom would have ever passed on, except for my pressing about her social life during college. Attending the University of Colorado in Boulder from 1925-1929, she joined a sorority and was active during her four years there. One day Mom chose to support a "sister" who had attempted suicide and was nearly drummed out of the sorority for her so-called "moral misbehavior."

Mom gave Maxine direct emotional help, but moreover, and here comes the act of justice, she spoke out during a secret sorority meeting when her beleaguered sister was being roundly condemned. Mom said: "Hey, sisters, if anyone should be standing on trial, it's probably you and me; for if we didn't fail Maxine along the way, we are certainly failing her now by condemning her to further misery through trying to vote her out of our sorority."

My mother's moral spine carried the day, and Maxine not only stayed in the sorority but was strongly involved in its very politics until her death, never knowing that her "beloved sorority" nearly took her pin away.

And what does God require of us but to do justice, then **"to love kindness."** In Jewish tradition it is voiced explicitly in an old proverb: "The highest form of wisdom is kindness." No footnotes or amendments need be made. Kindness is the final determiner of the merit of one's existence.

That's what social responsibility is all about, at its highest common denominator: being kind. When in doubt, be kind; when frightened, risk kindness; when bitter, speak kindly. Lovers empathize with the sentiment philosopher Aldous Huxley expressed when he wrote, "It's a bit embarrassing to have been concerned with the human problem all one's life and find at the end that one has no more to offer by the way of advice than this—'Try to be a little kinder.'"

"What does the Eternal require of you, but to do justice,

and to love kindness and **to walk humbly with your God**?"

What does humility have to do with loving? Everything! We need humility, since arrogance builds walls, not bridges, between individuals or clans. We need humility, since brash egos hanker for personal credit rather than shared accomplishment. We need humility, since, although human beings are marvelous works of art, we are neither the Infinite One nor the centerpiece of creation.

As lovers committed to being shameless agitators for justice and kindness, we must walk humbly with ourselves, with our neighbors, and with all living things. Additionally, we are called neither to walk in front of God in haughtiness nor behind in servility but alongside as bona fide partners in the interdependent web of all existence. And notice that Micah directs us to walk humbly with *our* God, not somebody else's.

But walking humbly doesn't allow us to wander off into apathy or laziness. Just because we can't do everything, it doesn't mean we can't do the things that you and I are peculiarly gifted and charged to accomplish. Just because we can't repay the Creation for its manifold blessings, it doesn't mean we must not respond to the Creation through deeds of justice and mercy. We must.

If not us, who? If not now, when?

XXX
FORGIVENESS

As much as religions teach that forgiveness is the bone-deep essence of faith, learning it is lifetime's lesson mastered by few. Grudge-bearing skills are applauded, not those of personal clemency. Governments have departments of justice, not departments of mercy. For individuals and nations, a change of heart is difficult enough. Forgiveness demands a change in thinking.

Colman McCarthy

Forgiveness is our deepest need and highest achievement.

Horace Bushnell

Forgiveness is life's invitation to redeem failure. It allows love to begin again. The Old Testament view of forgiveness is contained in a verb that pervades its penitential literature, namely, the Hebrew word: **shuv**, meaning "to turn, to return." This biblical doctrine of forgiveness is eminently hopeful, forecasting our human ability to turn from evil to good, from alienation toward reconciliation.

Without the blessing of forgiveness, we are never released from the consequences of what we have done or what has been done to us. We remain enslaved. As Reinhold Niehbuhr notes: "Forgiveness is the final form of love." So it is—as well as probably love's most difficult treasure.

We humans are prone to bypass forgiveness, racing with lightning speed from our hurts to healing without taking a sober look at what must first be pardoned. Signed peace treaties are habitually broken before the ink is dry. Without forgiveness, there can be no real peace and no lasting reconciliation.

Forgiveness is an arduous, transformative process. Near the end of Gandhi's life, he went on another of his long and serious fasts in protest against Hindus and Moslems killing one another. Finally, they came to their senses and temporarily ceased the bloodshed.

Among those who begged Gandhi to end his fast was an agitated Hindu who confessed that in retaliation for the murder of his young son, he had smashed the skull of a Muslim's baby against a wall. Severely distraught over the absurd enormity of two innocent deaths, he asked Gandhi what he might do to redeem himself.

With that pragmatic bent typical of his moral genius, Gandhi, from his bed, urged the man to go find a Muslim youth, a boy about the same age as that of his dead child, and to raise him like a son, but in the Muslim, not the Hindu, faith. Genuine redemption demands behavioral change, often extraordinary sacrifice.

While not overlooking ugliness and fracture, forgiveness charges us to surrender resentment and to forfeit pride. Forgiveness may be excruciatingly demanding and costly (it may even prove unworkable in certain situations), but the evidence shows that non-forgivers pay a more severe emotional price in refusing to risk restoration. For those who will not forgive have destroyed the very bridge over which they themselves must pass on the road to responsible freedom and new creation.

Forgivers recognize that our common humanity transcends national fervor, holy crusades, or enemy status. There is an inconvenient phrase tucked away in the celebrated 23rd Psalm that nudges us to be reconcilers and reconciled: "Thou preparest a table before me in the presence of my enemies." Now, setting a table before family or friends hardly poses a lover's challenge, unless, of course, we are at odds with our own kin. But being prodded by God to be companions with our foes, literally, to break bread with our enemies, constitutes an extreme order of love.

At core, forgiveness indicates the refusal to demonize our opponents, for only in the give and take of relational compassion is it possible to build a world that both we and our foes can affirm. It lies within enlightened self-interest to love our enemies, for we and our rivals share in common inconsolable pain, the certainty of dying, as well as the gift of this sole, precious earth. Knowing all that should, and thankfully often does, drive us toward a truce.

Breaking the cycle of violence requires remembering that real human beings reside on the other side of any hostility. No one on earth is expendable wherever they live, whatever system they espouse, no matter what they have or haven't done.

There is a rabbinical legend that portrays God as chastising the angels of heaven who want to exalt God with ecstatic hymns of thanksgiving when the waves of the Red Sea close over the drowning Egyptians. "My creatures, the Egyptians, are perishing and you want to sing praises!" God's mercy is too often exceeded by our revenge. We selfishly strive to be favorites, when God's love transcends partiality and ideologies.

To implement the forgiving process there are a few proven reminders.

First, forgiveness is not a single act so much as a constant attitude. The scribes in the Bible taught that one should forgive three times. Peter was generous and suggested seven times. Jesus came along and said: "Seventy times-seven" (Matthew 18:22) which, of course, goaded us to quit keeping score and stick to forgiving.

Second, if we need and want to forgive, we should go ahead and do so. It isn't necessary to tell the person we are forgiving that they are the subject of our efforts. The same rule obtains after forgiveness occurs. We have no obligation to tell the people we have forgiven that we have done so. Sometimes it helps, often it doesn't. Forgiveness doesn't have to be reciprocal in order to prove beneficial to ourselves.

Third, forgiveness is just as hard to receive as to give. Forgiveness is difficult to give because we need to see the one who hurt us as other than the hurt, and that isn't easy. Forgiveness is difficult to receive because we need to believe that someone has seen more in us than the hurtful thing we did.

Fourth, it is never too late or impossible to forgive. It took twenty-five years before Michelangelo could forgive a rival for deliberately defacing a set of his drawings. The cruelty associated with that act of vandalism drove Michelangelo into a lengthy depression. By the time he was finally able to forgive, the man who had committed the act was already dead.

Fifth, both large and small hurts (whether the break-up of a friendship or the slight of a salesclerk) are matters for forgiveness. We stay in practice by repairing every shape and size of brokenness.

Sixth, there is no **one** way to forgive. Even the biblical strategies vary from turning the other cheek to confronting those who have wronged us. It all depends on the situation and the people involved. But the same motivation universally applies: to set enslaved people free, both forgiver and forgiven.

Finally, who needs to be forgiven? The list is endless, and all our names are on it. We need to forgive institutions and countries, our own as well as foreign ones. God could use human forgiveness too. Most critically, we need to forgive ourselves. Francis of Assisi called this, "loving the leper within us." Whatever blunder or failure or sin we have committed, it is only a part of who we are. We need to forgive ourselves, because we will never be able to receive another's forgiveness, God's included, unless we do.

Forgiveness is a sublime and difficult enterprise, an adventure not much in fashion nowadays. Yet given the alternatives of avoidance, revenge, or forgiveness, the latter is the only option that brings our lives its needful release and refreshment over the long haul. Forgiveness is the power that saves us from decay, the hope that overcomes haunting despair, the love that frees us from consuming acrimony.

XXXI

ALWAYS GREEN AND FULL OF SAP

Do not say 'Why were the former days better than these?' For it is not from wisdom that you ask this.

Ecclesiastes 7:10

Life has been described as a play with a lousy third act. The way to deal with it is not by changing the plot, that's inevitable, but by changing the characters.

George Sheehan

Age puzzles me. I thought it was a quiet time. My seventies were interesting, and fairly serene, but my eighties are passionate. I grow more intense as I age. To my own surprise I burst out with hot conviction.

Florida Scott-Maxwell

Lovers are bent on developing character and graying gracefully all the way home. They are unwilling to disappear during life's third act. They keep their embrace wide open. They exude "the gift of intelligent rage," knowing what things to fight and what things to disregard. When Rabbi Salman Schachter-Shalomi is confronted with someone moaning about getting old, he exhorts them "to shift from aging to **saging**, which entails acting as guide, mentor, and agent of healing and reconciliation on behalf of the planet, nation, tribe, clan, and family—becoming wisdom keepers."

There are several habits that keep us green while graying, on the course of saging rather than merely aging.

First, it is tempting to narcoticize ourselves with medicine or idleness rather than focus on interests of note and challenges of magnitude. Bingo may suffice as an intermittent diversion but not as a fulfilling activity for elders. One of the ways we stay spirited is by undertaking tasks of worth—not to earn money or applause but to enhance our soul during life's final laps.

In the suffragist and abolitionist era, women such as Sojourner Truth and Clara Barton remained enterprising well into their senior years. In large measure, these feminists lived energetic, lengthy lives because they were occupied with moral challenges. They kept harvesting until the end. They tracked Shakespeare's wisdom: "This is to be new born when thou art old, to see thy blood warm when thou feels't it cold."

Second, rather than living entrapped in sentimental bygones, persons graying gracefully focus upon the irrepeatable present. Countless adults hanker to be 12 or 25 or 48 once again when we are irretrievably 66 or 87. We would do well to follow the Jewish blessing: "Blessed be the Source of Life that brings us to **this** moment." Not yesterday or tomorrow but today. We must emotionally outgrow our past: its grudges and glories. If we are mentally beholden or romantically fixated on past loves (individuals, achievements, or dreams), we will never give ourselves entirely to living in the now. Graying lovers don't live *for* but *in* the present.

As Richard Gilbert wisely phrases it:

> *About the fact that I am getting older, there is nothing I can do. About how I am getting older, I can. This period of my life is the only time I have. So I can either stay in bed and complain or go out and pick daisies.*

Instead of looking back in nostalgia or ahead in anxiety, lovers of life look around and bask in current blessings. They mend broken bonds and update lagging interests. And they "go out and pick daisies," if that's what they really want to do!

There are surprises discoverable in every season of existence, the elder years included. Tyrannized by ambition and speed, we younger travelers ignore wonders circulating amidst this majestic creation. As we age and quit climbing, we can actually slow down and appreciate the beauty in which our lives are immersed. Gloria Wade-Gayles goes to the heart of the matter:

> *Becoming older is a gift, not a curse, for it is that season when we have long and passionate conversations with the self we spoke to only briefly in our younger years.*

Third, the elder epoch is the time to take chances. The Canadian novelist Robertson Davies claimed that the finest gift we can exhibit during our senior years is curiosity: "Curiosity about something. Enthusiasm. Zest. That's what makes old age a delight. One has seen so much, and is eager to see more." He liked to say: "You're not getting older, you're getting nosier." When we are young, we yield to noisiness; when we are older, we can focus on nosiness!

Pianist Arthur Rubinstein was once asked: "Am I right in thinking that you're playing better now than ever before?" "I think so," he answered. "Is it experience, practice, what?" "No, no, no," said Rubinstein, "I am 80. So now I take chances I never took before. You see the stakes are not so high. I can afford it. I used to be so much more careful, no wrong notes, few bold ideas, watch tempi. Now I let go and enjoy myself, and to hell with everything except the music!"

Life may be more uncertain and health less stable, but expectations and pressures are lifted in our saging years so we can become curious, nay brazen, adventurers. We have earned the right to be freer and fiercer.

When we retire (or "graduate from work" as one teenager

mused), it is not the time to lie fallow but the season to explore fresh realities—perhaps gardening around church grounds, tutoring at schools, taking up bird-watching, or assisting our grandchildren in their maturation.

Most of all, it's time to do what we really want to do. Sam Levenson said that when he was a boy he used to have to do what his father wanted, and then, as a parent, he had to do what his children wanted. When did he get to do what he wanted? That's a fair question, and the answer is: the elder years comprise, at long last, the season to do what Sam Levenson truly wants to do!

Fourth, growth is the only evidence of life. An elder American poet was asked how he kept young in spirit, and he pointed to the cherry tree in blossom, asking in turn, "Where are the blossoms?" The answer was, "On the new wood." It's the young branches that have the blossoms and bear fruit. The tree keeps on going by growing new life.

Lovers stay growing to the end, because we wish to suck life dry of its juices and richness. We stay forever young by forever learning. Justice Holmes was 92 when President Roosevelt asked him why he was reading Plato. He replied: "To improve my mind, Mr. President!" A member of our congregation in Davenport, Iowa, Alice Braunlich, in her late eighties started reading Russian novels and studying chemistry to fill in the gaps of her knowledge. She would also write critical comments in the margins of my printed sermons and pressure me to go over them with her.

One of my favorite scriptures on maintaining an evergreen awareness is Psalm 92:14: "In old age they still produce fruit; they are always green and full of sap." Our final laps should in fact be generative ones, "always green and full of sap," at least *usually* green and full of sap. However, for that to happen, we have to stay buddha-like or "awakened" to the end.

Erik Erikson says that the final life-crisis revolves around "integrity versus despair." Integrity means displaying wholeness and embodying dignity during our closing laps. During the second half of what Jung calls the afternoon of existence, there will be numerous stinging losses to face. Our children leave the nest, our parents and good friends die. Integrity denotes the spiritual capacity to move resiliently amid both the grievous and triumphant moments of life's homestretch.

Integrity enables us to review the total record during our one trek on this planet: our blunders, our brilliance, and our blahs. Integrity also acknowledges that while each of us is irreplaceable, none of us is indispensable.

An addendum to the saying, "We live only once," might be: "If we live with integrity, once will be enough!"

XXXII
SHOUT AMEN!

> If there is a sin against life, it consists perhaps not so much in despairing of life as in hoping for another life and in eluding the implacable grandeur of this life.
>
> *Albert Camus*

> Our task is to say a holy yes to the real things of our life as they exist.
>
> *Natalie Goldberg*

> We cannot choose our mooring posts, our lovers, our friends any more than we can choose our parents. Life gives these to us, and the important thing is to say Yes to life!
>
> *James Baldwin*

There is a story told of geography students, having toured the earth by book, who were asked at semester's end to list what each considered the **Seven Wonders of the World**. Though there was some disagreement, the following garnered the most votes: Egypt's Great Pyramid, the Taj Mahal, Grand Canyon, Panama Canal, Empire State Building, St. Peter's Basilica, and the Great Wall of China.

While tallying the votes the teacher noted that one student, a shy girl, had not turned in her paper. "Did you have trouble?" the teacher inquired. "A little," the child replied, "I couldn't quite make up my mind, because there were so many."

"Well, tell us what you have, and maybe we can help," the teacher suggested. The bashful girl rose to her feet and began, "I think the "Seven Wonders of the World" are to touch and to taste, to see and to hear..." she hesitated, "and then to *run* and to *laugh* and to *love!*" Now, there's a youngster already awash with life's palpable splendor!

There are various sins we commit along the way: imitating someone else, fixating on the past, damaging those bonds we cherish, settling for shallow gratification, but the lover's overriding sin is scorning the riches of this priceless creation.

My father-in-law, a brilliant painter and consummate lover of life, said during his dying days: "I'm not afraid to die, I just hate to leave this life. I love it so passionately and have so many more things to do." Indeed, he painted up until the very moment when he could no longer lift his arms to do so.

Today's youth are encouraged to stand up for their own rights, to say NO to drugs, promiscuity, abuse—to go the way of their consciences rather than obey the whims of the crowd. It is also heartening to see adults learning to quit stultifying jobs, to abstain from negative habits, to resist wrongdoing, to prune cluttered lives. As Meister Eckhart understood: "The spiritual life is not a process of addition but one of subtraction." It is tantalizing, albeit delusive, to love so many things that our soul grows overpopulated.

I tire of the pervasive commercial hype in our culture that urges, almost demands, us "to have it all!" Hogwash. Lovers don't want to have or be it all. We could care less about lots of things. There are games that are ridiculous and attitudes that are rotten. The assignment for the loving adult is to make discriminating choices about what is needful and what isn't.

Arnold Bennett, author of *How to Live on Twenty-four Hours a Day*, was once confronted by a lady who gushed compliments about his book, "And now, thanks to you and your book," she gushed, "I am going to concentrate." Answered Bennett, "On what?" "Oh," said the lady, "on lots and lots of things!" She had clearly missed his point.

As loving elders our aim is to shed widely and focus deeply, ever emphasizing the primary theme of one's singular life. We cannot have it all without scattering ourselves to the wind. One wit described greed as chasing two hares at the same time, thereby having both elude our grasp.

However, all of our NOs must remain in service of the overriding behest of saying YES to life itself. We denounce in order to announce. We resist in the name of our affirmations. We protest (literally "testify on behalf of") something positive that we cherish. Our NOs pave the way for our predominant YES. A monk asked Joshu, one of the greatest Zen masters in China: "What is the one ultimate word of truth?" Without hesitation, Joshu responded, "Yes!"

The Creation is one lavish gift of prodigal proportions and possibilities beyond our deserving. Life offers us vast opportunities to use ourselves for mighty, not idle or trivial, purposes. The only soul-sized response we humans can make is to say Yes to life's call for truth, beauty, and goodness. A Yes that translates into Yeses where we give concretely of our time and our talents to those efforts we cherish.

The Talmudic tale reminds us that when Moses struck the Red Sea with his wand, nothing happened. The Red Sea opened only when the first person jumped in. Life opens up for us and those we love, when and only when, we take the plunge, saying Yes to life with every fiber of our body and soul.

Lovers advance to the state where they quit irresponsible naysaying and yes-butting and prefer to be carriers of a resounding Yes to life and all it's scary yet wondrous prospects. Lovers proclaim an unequivocal Amen to existence!

I grew up thinking that the term **Amen** meant "so be it," as if we were merely adding an exclamation point to what had just been spoken or sung in community. I have since learned that Amen correctly translates not "so be it" but "so *might* it be." Amen refers not to an actuality so much as a hope.

Therefore, whenever I voice an "Amen" in public, I am, in

effect, pledging to do everything possible to help my sentiment come true. Amen isn't another sweet superfluous four-letter word thrown in for magical measure. Amen is a promise to translate our yeses into deeds that heal and empower the cosmos.

XXXIII
STRONGER THAN DEATH

Lovers being full of life...are full of death. So deep is death implanted in the nature of love that...it nowhere contradicts love.

Rainer Maria Rilke

Who wields a poem larger than the grave? Love.

e. e. cummings

Love is God and to die means that I, a particle of love, shall return to the general and eternal Source.

Leo Tolstoi

Love is stronger than death.

Song of Solomon

We come of age when we grasp that every love relationship ends in a loss: through divorce, departure, or death. We will die and so will our comrades and loved ones. As we open ourselves to the precarious depths of love, we open ourselves to the raw anguish of loss.

Yet lovers experience those we have cherished living on in our souls after their earthly treks. Lovers contend, along with Ainnenap, the Shonshone medicine healer, "If the dead be truly dead, why should they be walking in my heart." Lovers stay connected with the land of the dead, the territory of the ancestors.

There is more. Just as we were loved into being beyond our earning, so also there will be Love attending us after we die. There is no need to discuss or debate the particular form such Love might take. No one knows. It is only important that we

116

declare with steady fervor and unshakable hope that the very Love that created us will caress us beyond our death...into illimitable seasons.

Robert Penn Warren in "Heart of the Backlog" offers life's ultimate query: "Is God's love but the last and most mysterious word for death?"

With quivering gratitude, lovers say Yes, Yes, Yes!

MORE QUOTES TO LOVE BY

There are bountiful quotations on the subject of love, un-doubtedly more than on any other life-theme, so I have narrowed the following assortment to those that pertain specifically to the vision of this book: the hard blessings of doing the work of love. Sprinkled throughout this word-feast are whimsical citations as well.

Most of these I have collected myself, from hither and yon, especially over the 33 years of my professional ministry. But two compilations have been fruitful: (1) *The Crown Treasury of Relevant Quotations* by Edward Murphy (1978) and (2) *The Beacon Book of Quotations by Women*, compiled by Rosalie Maggio (1992). My hope is the reader won't find all of these selections pleasing and congenial; if valuable, they should prove provocative enough to push your mind into irregular shapes and cause your heart some indigestion.

If I am to stay alive, I am bound to continue to get love wrong, all the time, but that is my life affair, love's work.

Gillian Rose

Love is a sacred reserve of energy; it is like the blood of spiritual evolution. This is the first revelation we receive from the sense of the earth.

Pierre Teilhard de Chardin

Intense love is often akin to intense suffering.

Frances Ellen Watkins Harper

Some love is very loud and noisy like a cage of monkeys, and other love hides away like a crab in the sand, afraid to show itself. We can never just walk up to somebody and say—love me the way I want to be loved. We have to wait for them to do it in their own way at their own time.

Thom Demijohn

Here I am at fifty-eight and in the past year I have only begun to understand what loving is...Forced to my knees and again like a gardener planting bulbs or weeding, so that I may once more bring a relationship to flower, keep it truly alive.

May Sarton

We are shaped and fashioned by what we love.

Goethe

Love is a choice—not simply, or necessarily, a rational choice, but rather a willingness to be present to others without pretense or guile.

Carter Heyward

Unarmed truth and unconditional love will have the final word in reality.

Martin Luther King, Jr.

Love is the vital essence that pervades and permeates, from the center to the circumference, the graduating circles of all thought and action. Love is the talisman of human weal and woe—the open sesame to every soul.

Elizabeth Cady Stanton

To cheat oneself out of love is the most terrible deception; it is an eternal loss for which there is no reparation, either in time or in eternity.

Soren Kierkegaard

I love you no matter what you do, but do you have to do so much of it?

Jean Illsley Clarke

And this I pray, that your love may more and more abound in knowledge and in all understanding.

Philemon I: 9

Love me in full being.

Elizabeth Barrett Browning

Not to think alike, but to love alike.

Francis David

You are here because somebody has loved you enough to make sure that you are here. You are paid for.

Maya Angelou

The question asked at the end of life is very simple: Did you love well the people around you, your community, the earth in a deep way?

Jack Kornfield

From suffering I have learned this: that whoever is sore wounded by love will never be made whole unless she embraces the very same love which wounded her.

Mechtild of Magdeburg

Everything flowers from within, of self blessing; though sometimes it is necessary to reteach a thing its loveliness...until it flowers again from within, of self blessing.

Galway Kinnell

I have found the paradox that if I love until it hurts, then there is no hurt, but only more love.

Mother Teresa

With the exception of only a few situations, there adheres to the tenderest and most intimate of our love-relations a small portion of hostility.

Sigmund Freud

The moment the system makes us hate other groups rather than love ourselves, it has won and we have lost.

Gloria Wade-Gayles

If you want a person to be your friend—don't do something for them, have them do something for you.

John Taylor

It was the kind of desperate, headlong, adolescent calf love that we should have experienced years ago and gotten over.

Agathie Christie

Love makes good thinking possible. If your heart is strong, you can have wise thoughts.

William Sloane Coffin

Love is like the measles. The older you get it, the worse the attack.

Mary Roberts Rinehart

Hate is love starved.

Kahlil Gibran

Love is not enough. It must be the foundation, the cornerstone—but not the complete structure. It is much too pliable, too yielding.

Bette Davis

May we be of equal affections, but if not, then may my love the greater be!

W. H. Auden

Let us make our gardens half artful and half wild, to match our love.

Marge Piercy

What is the purpose of love? No purpose. Love is its own reward.

Depra Choprak

There is always something left to love and if you ain't learned that, you ain't learned nothing.

Lorraine Hansberry

There is a single magic, a single power, a single salvation, and a single happiness, and that is called loving.

Herman Hesse

Partnership is marked by strange multiplication tables.

Letty Russell

Let yourself be silently drawn by the stronger pull of what you really love.

Rumi

Whoever said love conquers all was a fool. Because almost everything conquers love, or tries to.

Edna Ferber

Love does not dominate; it cultivates.

Goethe

If only one could tell true love from false love as one can tell mushrooms from toadstools.

Katherine Mansfield

There is only misfortune in not being loved; there is misery in not loving.

Albert Camus

To most people, love will always be more than the sum of its natural parts. It's a commingling of body and soul, reality and imagination, poetry and phenylethylamine. In our deepest hearts, most of us harbor the hope that love will never fully yield up its secrets, that it will always elude our grasp.

Hannah Bloch

The clear proof of a person's love of God is if that person genuinely shows love to fellow human beings.

Dalai Lama

We can say with conviction that anything our children love can be sheltered by their love; anything they truly love can be saved. First, in their own hearts, and then in the hearts of others.

Alice Walker

Love is at first not anything that means merging, giving over, and uniting with another...it is a high inducement to the individual to ripen, to become something in him/herself...

Rainer Maria Rilke

Where there is great love, there are always miracles.

Willa Cather

...faithful are the wounds of a friend.

Proverbs 27: 6

Make no judgments where you have no compassion.

Anne McCaffrey

Love which is the most difficult mystery, asking from every young one answers and most from those most eager and most beautiful...

Archibald MacLeish

We love because it's the only true adventure.

Nikki Giovanni

The love is from God and of God and towards God.

T. E. Lawrence

Love must be learned and learned again and again; there is no end of it. Hate needs no instruction, but wants only to be provoked.

Katherine Anne Porter

It is easy to love everyone when you don't have to be with anyone longer than a few minutes or hours. It is easier to hug a stranger, even taking into account the possibility of getting slapped for it, than to hug your spouse after he or she has criticized your personality or sexual prowess.

Bernie Zilbergeld

We cannot do great things. We can only do small things with great love.

Mother Teresa

There were rules in the monastery, but the Master always warned against the tyranny of the law. "Obedience keeps the rules," he would say, "while love knows when to break them."

Anthony de Mello

We've got to love each other enough to struggle with each other. If you want to build genuine community, then be ready to have your view of the world turned upside down and then right side up again.

Barbara Majors

When you get love, pass it on! Spend it, like money! Don't hoard it! Put the love you receive to work by investing it in other people.

Webster Kitchell

In real love you want the other person's good. In romantic love you want the other person.

Margaret Anderson

Love your enemies and pray for those who persecute you.

Matthew 5: 44

I believe that love is the single, true prosperity of any moment and that whatever and whoever impedes, diminishes, ridicules, opposes the development of loving spirit is "wrong"/hateful.

June Jordan

Love in practice is a harsh and dreadful thing compared to love in dreams.

Fyodor Dostoyevsky

Knowing that love is not a limited resource, not an endangered species, doesn't help at all. What does it matter if there is a vast ocean of love out there, if I'm not able to immerse myself in it; if I'm locked up in here, without a drop of that ocean's moisture to bless me?

Elizabeth Tarbox

Love means going to any length to restore broken community.

Martin Luther King, Jr.

The truth is that there is only one terminal dignity— love. And the story of a love is not important; what is important is that one is capable of love.

Helen Hayes

To reconcile conflicting parties, we must have the ability to understand the suffering of both sides. If we take sides, it is impossible to do the work of reconciliation.

Thich Nhat Hanh

How do I love thee? Let me count the ways. I love thee to the depth and breadth and height my soul can reach.

Elizabeth Barrett Browning

My bounty is as boundless as the sea, my love is as deep; the more I give to thee, the more I have, for both are infinite.

William Shakespeare

Love has a longitude and latitude all its own. So please don't go away again, for when you do, you change the degree of love between us.

Lois Wyse

Anyone can hate. It costs to love.

John Williamson

People talk about love as though it were something you could give, like an armful of flowers. And a lot of people give love like that—just dump it down on top of you, a useless strong-scented burden. I don't think it is anything you can give...love is a force in you that enables you to give other things. It is the motivating power.

Anne Morrow Lindbergh

"What is love?" "The total absence of fear," said the Master. "What is it we fear?" "Love," said the Master.

Anthony de Mello

Everyone wants Love to follow them down their roads; where is it that Love wants to go?

Judy Grahn

Love does not put everything at rest; it puts everything in motion. Love does not resolve every conflict; it accepts conflict as the arena in which the work of love is to be done.

Daniel Day Williams

To love deeply in one direction makes us more loving in all others.

Madame Swetchine

We cannot avoid using power, cannot escape the compulsion to afflict the world so let us, cautious in diction and mighty in contradiction, love powerfully.

Martin Buber

Great spirit...thank you again. I love you. I love your trees, your sun, your stars and moon and light. Your darkness. Your plums and watermelons and water meadows. And all your creatures and their fur and eyes and feathers and scales.

Alice Walker

Life has taught me, and this is my luck, that active loving saves me from a morbid preoccupation with the shortcomings of society and the waywardness of human beings.

Alan Paton

We women learn it at last—that the one gift in our treasure house is love, love, love. If we may not give it, if no one looks into our eyes and asks our gift—we may indeed collect ourselves and offer our second-best to the world, and the world may applaud. But the vital principle is gone from our lives.

Ruth Benedict

Love asks that we be a little braver than is comfortable for us, a little more generous, a little more flexible. It means living on the edge more than we care to. Love is always in danger of being the most painful single emotion we can ever feel, other than perhaps a sudden knowledge of our own death. La Rochefoucauld said that wonderful remark "that half the people in the world would have never fallen in love if they had not heard of the word." I think that most people I know, maybe three-quarters of the people I know, have never been deeply in love.

Norman Mailer

I know that there is a way to love that frees. I know that there is a way to love that gives life. I know this even though I have not witnessed such love.

bell hooks

But to love is quite another thing: it is to will an object for itself, to rejoice in its beauty and goodness for themselves, and without respect to anything other than itself.

Etienne Gilson

In the mystery of love, as you learn to love another truly, you find the Divine Lover revealed within that other human being.

Jean Houston

Animals are not our property or chattel, but our peers and fellow travelers. Like us, they have their own likes and dislikes, fears and fixation. Animals not only have biologies; they also have biographies. They are our spiritual colleagues and emotional companions. We know this to be true less through debate than through direct experience.

Gary Kowalski

I have a stinking hangover and don't speak on the ride back, don't even think much except to tell myself how much jabber there is in the name of love.

Lillian Hellman

We say love is blind, and the figure of Cupid is drawn with a bandage round his eyes. Blind: yes, because it does not see what it does not like; but, the sharpest-sighted hunter in the universe is Love...finding what it seeks, and only that.

Ralph Waldo Emerson

Love so seldom means happiness.

Margery Allingham

To be capable of giving and receiving mature love is as sound a criterion as we have for the fulfilled personality.

Rollo May

Love—bittersweet, irrepressible—loosens my limbs and I tremble.

Sappho

I love you with what in me is still changing, what has no head or arms or legs...

Robert Bly

Love is anterior to Life—Posterior to Death.

Emily Dickinson

Earth is our mother, but it is also our father; it is our brother and sister, partner, male as well as female...Earth is sexy, just as sex is earthy. Each of us is a landscape of plains and peaks, valleys and thickets. Body and land are one flesh. They are made of the same stuff.

Scott Russell Sanders

The emotion, the ecstasy of love, we all want, but
God spare us the responsibility.

Jessamyn West

They had lived together long enough to know that
love was always love, anytime and anyplace, but it
was more solid the closer it came to death.

Gabriel Marquez

This time I think I'll face love with my heart instead
of my glands. Rather than hands clutching to sati-
ate, my fingers will stroke to satisfy. I think it might
be good to decide rather than to need.

Nikki Giovanni

Love...a word I have uttered time and time again
and now hesitate to say at all—being, as it is, always too much to stand for what we really mean,
and never enough.

Michael Blumenthal

All shall be well, for there is a love that will not let
us go.

Julian of Norwich

To be loved for what we are, is the greatest exception. The great majority love in us only what they
lend us, their own selves, their version of us.

Goethe

Learning to love differently is hard—love with the
hands wide open, love with the doors banging on
their hinges, the cupboard unlocked...It hurts to love
wide open...

Marge Piercy

As an act of bravery, love cannot be sentimental; as
an act of freedom, it must not serve as a pretext for

manipulation. It must generate other acts of freedom; otherwise it is not love...

Paolo Freire

I go where I love and where I am loved, into the snow. I go to the things I love with no thought of duty or pity.

Adrienne Rich

There can be love in being told we are wrong. There can be love in sharing a regret. There can be love in asking for help. There can be love in communicating hurt. There can be love in telling hard truths. Most of us find it painful to live at this level of love, but it can be there, even in these most unlikely places.

David Blanchard

When someone says "I love you," they always ought to give a lot of details: like why and how much and when and where did they begin to love you?

Judith Viorst

The emotion of love, in spite of the romantic, is not self-sustaining; it endures only when the lovers love many thing together, and not merely each other.

Walter Lippman

It is more interesting, more complicated, more intellectually demanding and more morally demanding to love somebody. It's so uninteresting to live without love. Life has no risk. Love just seems to make life not just livable, but a gallant, gallant event.

Toni Morrison

I, here and now, finally and forever, give up knowing anything about love, or wanting to know. I believe it doesn't exist, save as a word: a sort of wailing phoenix that is really the wind in the trees.

D. H. Lawrence